Welcome

This book tells a story. It's the story of every entrepreneur and senior leader in business.

I've interviewed founding entrepreneurs and leaders and you can read what they had to say, in full and in their own words, about the highlights and lowlights, what they learned and how they got out of their own way and reshaped the business when necessary in order to survive.

You'll find many lessons learned that will resonate with you if you're trying to successfully grow your business and are open to learning from those who have been there and done it. Take the parts of the story that are familiar to you, understand the personal learning that made the difference for others, and ask yourself, 'How can I use that?'

To your success.

Angela Dellar

Table of Contents

Peter Jarvis: "Be the leader you want to work for" 5

Rowan Gormley: "Ask, don't tell, if you really want your business to grow" 22

Dr Louise Beaumont: "David vs. Goliath looks like a fair fight in comparison" 33

Alan Ridealgh: "Be true to yourself and people will follow" 48

Russ Stilwell: "Live your values" 62

Angus Thirlwell: "If you want a sustainable, profitable business, get a bit of brand WOW!" 78

Keith Paxman: "Don't be fearful... grasp the opportunity and run with it" 104

Angela Dellar: "Keep it simple" 117

About the Author 132

Thank you's 134

Copyright notices 137

Legal notices 138

Peter Jarvis: "Be the leader you want to work for"

Contechs was founded in Essex in 1997 and initially focused on supplying CAD services to Ford and a number of automotive suppliers.

It achieved steady, organic growth, extending its engineering services and making a series of strategic business acquisitions.

Contechs opened its current office in Basildon in 2002, by which time it had added materials handling programmes to its portfolio. In 2003 it acquired the Hawtal Whiting business and brand from Wagon Group plc, a Tier 1 supplier of design, engineering and recruitment services to Jaguar Land Rover.

Led by a senior management team of industry specialists, it has built up sector-leading experience in CAD and engineering services, delivering consistent, efficient services across the full range of vehicle development, from design concept origination to product launch and post-launch support.

Hi Peter and welcome. Thank you for being involved. Please could you give us some background about yourself, Contechs and your story to this point?

So, I am the Managing Director and one of the owners of Contechs which has been in existence since 1997. We're proud to have achieved year-on-year growth even through recessions, and I think the way we've done that is by being very conscious about having scalable solutions so that we expand, but also contract, in a controlled way, if that makes sense. It's not about over-expanding in the good times. It's about doing it in a calculated way so that we are always able to be mindful that the world is not always going to be growing. You can still expand your profitability when you are retracting turnover.

I myself did an apprenticeship in aerospace and then very quickly after I finished with British Aerospace went to Landrover, where I went into the automotive industry, so I've worked for large and smaller suppliers meaning I've got a wide spectrum of experience in manufacturing and product development. I was quite conscious that I wanted experience of both so I had knowledge of the concept of a vehicle all the way through to the production of it and the whole process in between.

And that desire for continuing my education continues to this day. From the ages of 16-42 I've not stopped learning, going to technical college, university, I have teacher training certificates, two degrees, been on courses to learn bricklaying... I have that drive and that will to learn and then use my education to take things forward and I think that's really important and says something about my character really.

It's about doing things in a controlled way and I think that's what Contechs is. We've got a lot of liquidity in the business, no real major debts at all, and we're growing. Last year we turned over £36 million, 2015 we're projecting £43-44 million and then in 2016 we're looking at £50-55 million. We're now a European business and we made an acquisition last year in Germany. We also do joint projects in India and China. We have to come up with a lot of innovation. We've got to be dynamic, flexible, lean and nimble and always attract and present new services and ways of working to keep us in front of our competitors. That innovation and learning has really put us in good stead because we're only as good as we are because of the people that we employ, and we're really into pushing, training and developing those people and adding clear visions, goals and objectives that are then cascaded down to everyone. Therefore all employees have KPIs and I'll go through and review them personally as well so that we've got alignment from the directors to the board, all the way through the business.

You mention that word there, alignment, where everyone and everything is pulling together. It sounds like you really emphasise that...

Yes, 100%. That is really important as it gives people a sense of wellbeing. It's about the team and rewarding people as well. We do a lot with bonuses within the business and if we can't measure and control and monitor things then those bonuses aren't paid out accurately. We make sure that as the business grows, the individuals get rewarded for the growth of the business. The individual wins, therefore the business wins too, and that's the secret for a deliverable day-to-day job for the client.

Could you elaborate a little more on the importance of the wellbeing of your people?

We're about making decisions in a fast and nimble way. Some of those decisions might not always be right, but at least we're making them at a senior level and we're doing it when we need to do it so that the business is not held up by the managers, but we like our managers to come to us with different ideas. We'll take those ideas and we'll make commercial sense and evaluate them, and if they do make sense, we'll implement and empower the managers that came up with the idea to go and do it and we'll fund it. It's like new ways of learning. At Contechs we're setting up academies and all those ideas now are self-generated from the managers in the business, and even some of the more junior people as well. It's about finishing ideas and then from those ideas the business flourishes.

As you say, those ideas come from people who are doing it daily and can see exactly what needs to be done and what would benefit from improvement.

Yes, we've gone from pushing the business to now being pulled along by the business as it goes past a critical size, but the problem I've always had is I've got so many ideas that come to me from various routes that we can't fulfil them all. So, the important thing is not trying to reinvent the wheel. We've had a go at that in terms of new initiatives, but we need to focus on core competencies and there are some good ideas where you can still push the boundaries, but don't break them. Don't go off and start thinking you're going to make millions on a brand new idea – make sure that it complements your core business and core competencies.

You talk about a key success factor being growth in a controlled manner and in a way that complements the core of what you do. Extensions of existing or evolution of what you have, rather than revolution – is that it?

Yes, that's exactly right. I think any business or entrepreneur needs to know their market and the size. There's a range, a peak and a trough, and you need to be aware of what that is and where you can operate. You see a lot about competitors over-expanding and when the bad times come again then you'll see those companies having serious problems. So, we've spent a lot of work focusing on controlled growth. Getting to our £50-55 million and then not really becoming a lot bigger in terms of turnover, but instead maximising profitability and value and then being more selective about the types of work that we want and turning the work away that we don't. To me, that's what good looks like, it really is.

What do you believe is the key to being able to up the ante, increasing profitability whilst running with the same turnover?

I think the big one for me is IT and specialists, and that comes back to excellence in people. We've got some real specialists in that area and we're recruiting some real heavyweights, so it's about recruiting the right people on a continual basis to really ensure that you are more knowledgeable than the manufacturers themselves in certain areas. You've got a real speciality that sets you apart and that clients always want to tap into.

You're 'extra special' and 'extra different' in terms of your specialist knowledge from the skills that your people bring and can then be niche as a result...

Yes, exactly. I think what we've been bad at – and I think it's important that we acknowledge weaknesses because I think that's a good way to look at things and then correct them when you can – is that we've never been very good at doing what we're doing now in terms of promoting ourselves, talking about us. We've always been very modest and very quiet so we've grown behind the back door, if that makes sense. Now what we've got to do is get more press coverage and PR coverage and tell people about who we are because our clients expect that from a business that we are now the size of. We need to be more out there and that again will also increase sales up to our target and enable profitable growth for us.

Is it fair to say that the business needs you out there doing the PR at the size it is now?

Yes, that's a very fair comment. I think we are determined and I suppose that comes from me. It is about hard work and drive really. I suppose it's a bit like being the captain of a ship; you've got to be there, you've got to be seen to do the right thing and lead from the front, rather than having a business that is a honeymoon type business. It's not about that. It's about hard work and all being in it together.

As with any senior leader within a company, your characteristics have positively shaped the culture, the 'way we do things around here': hard work, drive, determination, learning, growing and evolving together by working collaboratively in partnership with people. During your journey, was there a point where you thought 'something's got to change here'?

Last year and now this year. It's all about processes, documentation and procedures, and making sure that we are really slick in what we do. In any business, when you're focusing on delivering the job itself, when you've got so much change going on, if you're not careful you can lose control in terms of being aligned to each other. One of the big things that I did last year and am continuing with this year is to drive processes through the businesses, making sure that the KPIs cascade down to key managers and then for their staff, so that they understand that they have to fit in to the overall quality manual. That's quite easily forgotten if you're not careful and it's just about coming full circle back to what you do to ensure that you're always in control. The only way of doing that is by quality processes and procedures. I think that's a big one that a lot of organisations forget about when they go through a transition of growth.

We've come back to consistency again. Those processes are absolutely key in terms of everyone doing the same thing, knowing what needs to be done and how it needs to be done to ensure that the consistency is there, but also that it's scalable.

Exactly. I always say that it's a bit like buying a house. Buy a house to sell a house, if that makes sense. That's exactly the same with scalability. We should not be afraid of recession, the people that are afraid of it are the ones that don't plan for it and we need to accept that there will be other hard times because we're in one of the most competitive environments in the automotive industry. It's always gone up and down, so we plan the way we do business to take that into account. That's why we've got a lot of liquidity in the business. We could quite easily take that out if we wanted to, but we want to make sure that it's there for if we need it on a rainy day.

It's also about diversification of the business to de-risk it. Having come from an automotive background, I understand the peaks and troughs.

What was the catalyst for your realisation about processes last year?

I think as I see it, we were in danger of being busy and I was starting to get a little bit concerned by some of the things that were starting to happen. It was a case of just stopping where we were, aligning ourselves, and then we'll go forward in a controlled way. We needed to do that at the time because if you're not aware of that then you can implode and we've always grown in a very controlled way, which we're very proud of.

So, I think that's a big one for us really. If we were all on one site it would be easier, but we're not. We've got a site down in Basildon now, two new buildings down there that we bought last year, and we've got a place in Germany and offices in India as well. We've got to be really mindful that we're all on the same dance floor, because it's already much more difficult than if we were all located on one site.

What else is important because of the added complexity of operating from multiple sites?

Communication is massive as well and it starts from the top with a town hall sort of communication from me, and then the senior managers/directors will also do their communications, and that goes down and we need to ensure that we continue to do that because that is really the food for the individuals that are doing all the work. They need communications to know what's going on.

I'm noticing your language and how passionately you come across when you say 'it's food for individuals' and talk about individual wellbeing. It sounds like you've got a real appreciation for the fact that there are certain things that people need in order to perform well.

I think it's how you're brought up or what your beliefs are, but it's about treating people how you want to be treated yourself. I've seen these *Dragons Den* people on the TV, but I don't like the way that some talk to people. I know it's on the TV, but it really gets me how they talk to them as if they are better than the individuals that are coming on with their ideas. To me those ideas should be thought through and encouraged, and not dismissed in the way that they are sometimes. I think that's just the TV and press to be fair about it all.

So, you're passionate about treating others with respect and that then shapes how you treat others. That's an absolute key trait of an authentic leader. On the subject of leadership, the growth of the business will have required you to grow your leadership skills and change the role that you play. What have you done to equip yourself during that journey?

I'm very mindful that I'm one person in Contechs and as I get older I'm starting to notice I'm getting tired. The problem that I have, if I'm honest with myself, is that I'm a perfectionist and have always had great determination. Like with getting my degree, not just getting the degree, it's about having the best degree.

My way of thinking now in terms of what we're doing with fellow directors is to put a stronger management team together so that they run the business and we then are able to stand back more and just get involved when needed. It's about making that transition so we've been invited on a 365 accelerator programme for leading SMEs in the UK. It's basically a coaching for businesses and leading SMEs. Myself and Ian Brooks, my business partner, go to that quarterly and that's about achieving alignment with our own individual wants, needs and desires as well as the business's.

Stepping back is not about us all giving up and running away to the beach. It's about us saying OK, let's plan for three years, lets plan for six years and nine years, so that when we get through these different milestones, we make a choice as to what we do in the business. Our view is to grow the business, grow the team, empower the individuals, give more accountability, more bonus payments and as they get better, the business will be pulled along because we've got stronger people.

When you go from a small business to an intermediate size business, sometimes even though there are some good people, some of those people that you thought were good get overtaken by the business, and all of a sudden they haven't got the experience that the business needs. You have to recognise that. You can do that by topping up with training, but you also sometimes have to recognise that that individual just can't go to the next level, and that's where you bring people in to then give that specialist support and advice to take it forward, whilst still valuing the existing people.

The second layer is essential to the long-term sustainability of the business...

Yes, and so many business owners and entrepreneurs think they know everything. I'm one guy. I don't know everything and there's always someone out there that's going to know more, and it's about that mind-set and always about not getting too big for your boots.

As a leader, your key beliefs of 'treat people how you'd like to be treated', 'keep your feet on the ground', 'don't get too big for your boots' and 'be appreciative that others also have a lot to add' sound like they have served you well.

I'm quite process-orientated and I've got an engineering background. I always have to reflect back on that and it's all about models from education – strategy models, what worked and what didn't work. So, I have to walk between an academic world and an industrial world whereas if I just had an industrial world, I'd be thinking and be worried about making too many mistakes. So, it's about trying to get the balance between the two so that you can minimise the amount of mistakes you actually make.

We have a strong relationship with Coventry University. We involve them on a lot of new technology systems, processes and procedures, and we want their advice and we get some of the graduates in to work with us doing special assignments over a two-year period. It's about making sure that the culture of learning and new processes and technology is incorporated within us as a company going forward.

Your passion comes through and is great business sense. You mention process, your engineering background and your people being key. I always consider process as being the logical and rational and the people as the emotional and behavioural. Is there anything you would share around how you have to be mindful of both dynamics in the growth of the business?

I would say the key thing is always keep an open mind and discuss things objectively. If you've got a new initiative/idea, then come up with the objective data, present it and then we'll talk. It's not about having a chat for a chat's sake. We need substance to be able to give birth to something new, if that makes sense. If we haven't got a substance to make a value decision on then you're going to get the wrong decision being made.

Someone said to me you can't be taught to be an entrepreneur and they're right, it happens within you. Sometimes you wonder why are you like you are because you look around your family and friends and you question why are you the only one that seems to be doing what you're doing. The way that you think and continuously drive yourself can be a lonely place when you're there because it takes over and you have to be mindful of when to stop. Again, this comes back to what is the objective and know what it is when you start out.

It sounds a bit like being the only left-handed person when everyone else is right handed. It's that appreciation that you are different and you think differently and that that's a good thing for an entrepreneur.

It really is, but you haven't got to be the cleverest person in the world. You've got to have a degree of intelligence, but the cleverest people that went to my school aren't necessarily entrepreneurs or successful business-people. They've got good jobs, but it's really unusual how sometimes the cleverest people are not the ones that are the most successful people.

I'd suggest that your growth mind-set has a lot to do with that. You're always wanting and willing to learn new things. If you only had half a minute, what one piece of advice would you give to business owners out there?

Don't bite off more than you can chew and go into things knowing what you're going into. Don't, whatever you do, over-commit to the bank. I think you've really got to understand what you're going into nowadays because there aren't loads of people out there willing to help you anymore. You can be a really good business, but if you haven't got cash flow and if you haven't got liquidity you can nose-dive really easily and overtrade. So, it's about always keeping your feet on the ground and taking calculated risks, and I underline calculated.

Sound data and evidence to support your decisions is really vital...

Yep, the big thing is that you've got a real responsibility for the wellbeing of the people that work for you. They look at you and they want wages and regular payments. They've got wives, families, children and everything else. That is a real responsibility that collectively, industrial leaders of the UK really need to get to grips with. I think there's lot of good leaders out there, but some are just out for themselves. We are definitely here to look after the people that work for us and making the right decisions, taking calculated risk for the good of the collective.

Win-win by the sounds of it...

Yes, it is.

I suspect you have an extremely loyal employee base as a result.

Yes, we do.

That's the sort of stuff that connects to them and with them, from the heart.

If you asked me who do I respect out of all of the entrepreneurs in the world, I would say Richard Branson. I think what he has got right is the team approach to everything and everyone that works for him. He keeps the same model in terms of a team approach in every venture that he does. He rewards individuals and people like to work for him.

Thank you very much, Peter.

In brief

The world won't always be growing. Be very conscious about having scalable solutions so that you can both expand and contract in a controlled way. It's not about over-expanding in the good times; it's about doing it in a calculated way.

Always attract and present new services and ideas. This will ensure that you always keep ahead of your competitors. Be open to ideas being generated by everyone in your company, but have a clear evaluation process so that you pursue the right ones.

The success of your company is directly related to those you employ. Train and develop your staff and add clear visions, goals and objectives. Cascade them down through the organisation to achieve alignment.

Ensure that as your business grows, individuals get rewarded for the growth of the business too. The individual wins, therefore the business wins too.

Be bold with new ideas, but ensure that it complements your core business and core competencies. Know your market and the size. It's cyclical so there's a range, a peak and a trough, and you need to be aware of what that is and where you can operate.

Communication is key and it needs to start from the top and cascade down through the organisation. People need good communication to know what's going on and it makes them feel valued as an individual.

To grow the business, grow the team. Empower people, give them more accountability, more opportunity for reward and, as they get better, the business will be pulled along because it has stronger people.

Don't bite off more than you can chew and know what you're going into. Never over-commit to the bank. You can be a really good business, but if you haven't got cash flow and if you haven't got liquidity, your fortunes can easily nose-dive. It's about always keeping your feet on the ground and taking calculated risks.

Rowan Gormley: "Ask, don't tell, if you really want your business to grow"

Rowan Gormley is one of the UK's most successful serial entrepreneurs and, like all successful entrepreneurs, has collected some scars along the way which ultimately have helped him to achieve his success.

Rowan qualified as an accountant, but hated it so much that he left the day he could. He had always wanted to start his own business and very early on in his career he met Richard Branson, who gave him a job and enabled him to start a business too.

In 1995 and in just ten weeks Rowan, Jayne-Anne Gadhia, Tony Wood and "a bunch of nutters" set up Virgin Money which floated on the stock market for £1.2 billion.

From Virgin Money, Rowan then set up the Virgin One bank account and in 2000 set up Virgin Wines with Laura Knight and his brother Clinton. Virgin Wines was sold to a competitor in 2008, after which Rowan founded Naked Wines. [Shortly after this interview, Naked Wines was bought by Majestic Wines and Rowan was appointed as Chief Executive of Majestic Wines.]

Hi Rowan and thank you for your time today. Tell us how you came to be here.

The reason I left Virgin Wines was that they fired me. Not Virgin, but the people we sold it to. So, it was quite a traumatic event, but actually it turned out to the best thing that ever happened to me.

After I got the boot, 17 other people resigned. So, we had the opportunity to set up a completely new wine company, but it was in 2008 which was obviously a pretty scary time to be doing anything because the whole world was collapsing around our ears. But this was with a group of people who were really new and excited by it. So, in many ways, it was just a fantastic chance.

We were lucky in that we raised funding very quickly, which enabled us to get started, and, because it was a completely new venture, we were able to look at the business in a completely new way. Instead of just setting up another wine retailer, we really focused on solving a problem.

What problem was that?

The problem is that the two people in the wine business that count, the wine maker and the wine drinker, they're both getting screwed and all the people in the middle are making all the money. It's not that anyone is being criminal, it's just that it's an incredibly inefficient market. So, what we wanted to come up with was a business where the wine drinker and the wine maker both got a better deal and we built a business that could make money, while still achieving that. So, rather than making money at the expense of suppliers or customers, we wanted to create a virtuous circle, where everyone was better off.

The virtuous circle model that we eventually came up with is that we get our customers to invest in our wine makers and, because our customers help our wine makers by providing them with funding, our wine makers don't need to waste their time and money selling back to those customers. Which in turn means they can give them better wine for less money. The customers get reward for investing with access to delicious wines they simply wouldn't be able to buy any other way. And they get to do it at a price that is affordable to normal people, but they're drinking wines that rich people drink. The end result of the customer proposition is that you no longer need to be rich to drink great wine.

For the wine makers, it is your opportunity to make your wine the way you want to make it, without necessarily having to learn how to become an international businessman.

I'm hearing a lot in your story around integrity?

Yes, that's absolutely right. The reason we're called Naked is we figured out that if we're going to get people to fund wine makers they've never heard of, to make wines they've never tasted, they really had to be able to trust. The wine drinkers needed to trust the fact that the money was going to go there, the wines were going to be OK and, if they weren't, we would sort it out and just refund their money.

So, we had to be completely transparent. The customer had to be able to meet the wine maker; they had to be able to talk to each other. It was no good us saying 'this wine is delicious.' They had to see that other customers thought that wine was delicious. What that means is you're pushing the power that companies normally try to hold onto themselves out to your suppliers and your customers. Perversely, I think we've landed up with a better company as a result.

That resonates a lot, in terms of win-win business.

Yes, exactly. That's exactly what we're trying to achieve. I think, you know, there's an old way of doing business which is in many industries, where someone is making money at the expense of someone else. We really wanted to try to turn that round, to be more of a 'making money *with* other people' and in a way that was collaborative.

It's not because – and we are nice people – it's not because we want to be nice, it's because we wanted to build a business which had really strong, long-term shareholder value. The best way to do that is you can't create long-term value if you're screwing your customers. At some point, it will bite you on the arse.

The idea of 'creating with' sounds very much a driver for you personally...

Yes, exactly. Well, it's worked really well. We've got 300,000, we call them Angels, who are people who invest in our wine makers. Last year we did something like €80 million in sales in our sixth year of business. We've passed the break-even point and we have a fantastic following from our customers.

As you say, really strong growth within that too...

Yes, exactly.

During your growth journey, were there points at which you were frustrated and, on reflection, were problems of your own making that you needed to see in a different way to unlock that forward motion?

Yes, you know, because you were creating a new kind of business, it was hard. When you went to the wine makers and said "What do you hate most about your job? All right, we can fix all of that for you." What amazed us was the number of wine makers who, when you were able to show them that you could fix their problem for them, they didn't want to know.

You think, well, you've just told me how much you hate the fact that you sell to an agent, who sells to a retailer, who then beats you up on price and then doesn't pay you what they agreed to pay you anyway. Yet when we offer you an alternative, you go "Oh, I'm not sure about that." So, that took a lot of understanding of how to deal with it. Curiously, with our customer-facing staff, one of the things we've really emphasised to them is we want customers to experiment and try different wines. That means if someone doesn't like it, just refund them.

Of course in most businesses, when a customer calls and says "I don't like the wine, I want my money back," they try and look after the company, rather than looking after the customer. So, it actually took quite a bit of energy from us to get our people to understand that by looking after the customer, they were looking after the company.

That frustration there, around enabling your people to put the customer in the middle, what was the 'eureka' moment for you personally, that enabled you to move beyond that?

I think that the biggest dawning realisation for me was that I couldn't tell people what to do. The realisation that I can't do everything myself and telling someone how to do their job wasn't an efficient way to get them to do their job, that I had to change the way I worked.

Moving from 'Here are the ten things you need to do, come back and tell me when you've done them,' kind of mode, through to a 'This is where we want to get to; you tell me how you want to get there.' Letting people – and forcing people – to figure it out for themselves which actually starts by taking much longer, but, of course, in the end produces much better results because everyone is far more motivated when they've built their own plan. They've got buy-in into the plan, they're far more responsible for the outcome.

So, that was a big behavioural change for me because when you start with a start-up, on day one I buy my wines, I write the copy, I design the website and I do all kinds of things I'm not qualified to do. Over time you had to get used to the idea that you had to get other people to do this and you had to get people who were better than you to do it better than you. That was more about sharing a vision and then standing back.

I suppose another thing – another big change for me – has been if someone wasn't quite nailing the job, I would tend to compensate by picking it up and doing it for them, but of course you can't do that beyond a certain point. I had to become much more structured about saying 'Here are my expectations and this is what you need to do to do this job.' Then, with people who were failing with it, helping them to understand why and where they were falling short and then working with them to sort that out or else get them out of the organisation. It was quite tough.

It is the willingness to have those honest conversations.

Yes. It's just confronting difficult situations really. The easiest thing to do is to let those things slide.

You're talking around what I call 'Letting Grow'. Letting go and sharing control and decisions to enable the team to step up and enable the business to grow. Moving from managing, which is typically a 'tell' to achieve a task, to leading. It's about enabling people to do it for themselves.

Yes, absolutely.

If you were boarding a plane in 30 seconds, what other advice would you give business owners who were looking to grow their business?

30 seconds; I like that! Confront your demons. I think the hardest thing for a business owner to do is to move away from the areas that they are comfortable in to the areas that are tough. I think generally businesses fail never for lack of hard work, never for lack of good intentions and, quite often, people know in advance the reasons why it's going to fail, but just didn't confront them.

It's about trusting yourself...

Yes. As an example of that, when we set up Virgin Wines I had two successful start-ups behind me so I was pretty convinced I was God's gift to start-ups. We started this business: internet, wine and Virgin. Three sexy words right there; what could possibly go wrong? But we had our proposition completely wrong.

We raised a pile of money at the height of the dotcom boom, blew it all, and had absolutely nothing to show for it. We were sitting in a situation where I really couldn't accept that I'd just got this wrong and we just kept pouring money down the drain instead of acknowledging we'd got it wrong and taking the remedial action. What eventually forced me to do that was running out of money. I wish I'd done it earlier.

Instead of desperately holding onto something that seemed like a good idea a few years ago, but hadn't worked, we said

'If we were the new management team coming in to run this business, what would we do?' As soon as we approached it from that completely fresh point of view, what we saw was selling big wine brands for slightly less than supermarkets wasn't a viable business.

What customers really wanted from us was access to smaller, artisanal wines. We had to dramatically slash our overheads and bootstrap the business. We did that, we turned it around and we built it back up again into a successful, profitable business, but I probably took a year longer to do that than I should have because I refused to confront the fact that I'd got it wrong.

Thank you for your openness. What was the key to you confronting that? What helped you?

Like I say, running out of money! Part of it was I had a team around me of very good people who'd actually been telling me the right things to do, but I'd struggled to come to terms with it. So, I was fortunate in that I didn't need to go and invent a new business, there were already people who were helping me to do that. I suppose it was those two, really.

The team around you and listening, being able to take that step back...

Yes, most definitely. Great. Thanks, Angela and all the best.

Thanks, Rowan. I really do appreciate it and I know that many other business owners will too.

In brief

You can't do it all yourself. Telling people what to do doesn't make them want to do it. When they feel that they have the control and the tools to work it out themselves they will put so much more in. It takes longer the first few times, but really pays dividends with motivation, buy-in and growth, both their own and that of the business, in the long term.

Moving from tell to ask is the key difference between managing and leading. When you tell you are managing the task. When you ask you are leading the person to grow their skills, be more self-sufficient and enabling them to support the growth of the business.

Confront your demons. Most people can tell you what's wrong in their business and they procrastinate and rationalise why they're not taking action to put it right. The health of your business, and often yourself, depends on your ability to confront your demons as a business owner. If you struggle, a good coach will help you learn to identify the actions you need to take and how to take them.

If you want long-term, sustainable business, make sure your business model is win-win, based on mutual trust and collaboration.

Anyone who loves great quality wine at wholesale prices and wants the opportunity to get under the skin of their wine by understanding where and how it's made and to meet the producers can find out more at the Naked Wines website www.nakedwines.com/angels. The video of the UK Tasting Tour gives a fantastic insight into how it works and what it's like to be part of the Naked Wines community.

Dr Louise Beaumont: "David vs. Goliath looks like a fair fight in comparison"

Dr Louise Beaumont explains how Alternative Finance was born and the scale of the task involved in growing a new industry to service the engine room of the UK economy, the country's SMEs.

Welcome and thank you for being involved. How did your journey begin?

I started work in my mid-twenties which is a little later than normal because I did an MA from St Andrew's University and then I did a PhD from Strathclyde Business School. So, I took a while to get into the workplace.

I did about eight years of hard labour for Capgemini which is an IT services company. For them, I did a variety of roles from earning my crust as a consultant to doing jobs which are broadly best described as business development, in as much as it's trying to understand where the marketplace is going, what services we need to deliver them, how you would market those, how you would sell those and productise them. Then, actually getting involved in the selling of them so you could see if they actually delivered any return on investment and whether we made any money or not. Then I moved to Siemens' IT Services division where I did more of the same, including getting involved in some of their biggest deals.

After that, really it was consultancy, setting up my own business, which makes it sound terribly grand, but it really wasn't. It was a very small consultancy called Vector which really was my vehicle for doing what I did. So, it was all of that stuff around business development, whether you want to be fancy and call that strategy or whether you want to call it sales or marketing or product design or delivery. Whatever you want to call it, it was that.

I developed relationships and won business from about seven or so of the world's largest blue-chip companies and my clients included Capgemini, Siemens, Hewlett Packard, Microsoft, Adobe, Logica and Vodafone.

Then I realised there was a huge gap in the world of SME finance when I sold a large project to Siemens and made two mistakes. My first mistake was to have plotted and inveigled my way onto the Siemens preferred supply list where I had no business being; my business was far too small. But, nonetheless, I'd sold my way onto the preferred supplier list so I could win projects from them. The problem with this was there was really one defining way in which you knew you were on the preferred supplier list and it was that they stopped paying you in 30 days and started paying you in 90 days. Effectively, you started subsidising their cash flow, all for the right to win business. Shocking.

Then I went and compounded the error by winning some business. It was quite a large piece of business and they wanted me to sub-contract all of the other people that were going to help deliver this project. Of course the sub-contractors wanted to get paid in 15 days or 30 days and I was only going to get paid in 90 days.

That sounds like a very large negative cash gap.

Yes. All for having won work via being a preferred supplier. So, it was a comedy moment. I thought 'I've got a problem now. What do I do?' I did what every other SME does. I went to the bank and worst of all I went to the bank in about 2007 where they were preoccupied with tanking the global economy. I asked for what every single SME asks for which is an overdraft and they said no. I asked for a loan and they said no.

Then they offered me this thing called invoice finance. It just seemed to be loaded up with every variety of fee and it seemed to be incredibly restrictive. There were up-front fees, annual fees, fees for using the service, fees for not using the service, fees for extending the service, fees for terminating the service. There was a facility ceiling which was low and just restricted my ability to actually use the service I was paying all these fees for.

There was a debtor concentration limit too. I had all these other clients and what the bank said to me was "You've got to sell us all your invoices except the Siemens ones." All my other customers paid me in 30 days. They were not the ones I had a problem with. I thought maybe they hadn't understood. I said "I don't have a problem with those. I have a problem with the payment terms of the Siemens invoices. So, I don't need you to buy all the other invoices, I need you to buy (effectively discount) the Siemens ones." They said "Oh no, but we can't do that because too much of your business is with Siemens."

What was that like?

It was ridiculous. It was just beyond parody, it was literally a farce. I just said "Well, there's no way I can buy this service from you because it just doesn't work." They were surprised, but nonetheless there's no point in buying a service which isn't fit for purpose. So, my learning on that was that banks have products which are developed for industrial revolution style companies; big companies who want big sums of money, for long periods of time, which can be secured on assets.

I was a teeny-tiny little business. I wanted a small sum of money for a small period of time and I had nothing on which to secure it, other than the trading record of my business and my pipeline. So, in this respect, I'm just like every other business which has been born in the last 20 or 30 years. The number of small businesses in the UK has tripled in the last 20 or 30 years. The vast majority of these new businesses are services businesses, so you might hear of these as called intellectual property businesses or knowledge economy businesses. What that means is at the end of the day the asset gets in the lift and goes home. There are few other assets.

90 per cent of SME lending is delivered by four banking groups. They're set up to lend to businesses from the industrial revolution, not the knowledge economy, so I thought 'Right, there's a problem and an opportunity too.'

At that point I got together with some friends of mine who'd been kicking this idea around and we decided that we were going to launch a business to help meet this SME finance gap which we duly went on to do. We launched the company, we built the technology and we grew the business. I grew it to £75 million traded in the first couple of years, the first two years in fact, which was good because it was an entirely novel way of doing invoice finance.

We secured investments from an institutional investor, for whom I now work, called GLI Finance. GLI Finance have investments in 19 SME alternative finance providers which between them deliver eight different types of SME finance on three continents, so the US, Europe and Africa.

The really interesting thing is the sheer number of challenges that are in your path when you're trying to disrupt an incredibly vested interest, namely traditional finance. It is an established fact, from the Bank of England's own statistics, that every quarter since 2009 bank lending to SMEs has declined.

I spot a real determination and tenacity. What skills and what tips do you have that have enabled you to achieve that?

I'm going to give you some answers which are counter-intuitive as well as some ones which, I suspect, are fairly standard. The real answer is a combination of bloody mindedness and stupidity on my part. It really does take those two characteristics. I'm sure there are some more, like you have to be very hard-working, you have to be diligent, you have to be thorough, you have to work with good people, all of those things. I'll come back to all of those points, because they are important.

My utter stupidity was that I failed to understand the size and scale of the task. If I had understood the size and scale of the task, I would have gone and done something easier. I was stupid; I didn't understand and I didn't know that I didn't understand. So, in the words of Donald Rumsfeld (United States Secretary of Defence), who said that there are known knowns, known unknowns and unknown unknowns, the size and scale of disrupting the established finance model for SMEs was an unknown unknown.

What's been the upside of that?

Tenacity, from our deciding to get this little start-up going all the way through to it being part of a much larger investment portfolio, in GLI Finance. Real tenacity and bloody mindedness.

This is such a block to the economic growth of the country given the main engine room of growth in the UK economy are SMEs. They deliver 50 per cent of our UK GDP. It's just shocking how fundamental they are to our economy and bank lending to them has declined by billions since 2009. This means that the engine room of the economy is not getting the fuel it needs. That means the economy isn't growing as fast as it should do, it means that companies aren't growing as fast as they should do and tax take isn't going up as fast as it should do.

The reality is the banks are less willing and less able to lend to these smaller companies. Less willing because regulation has come in since the inter-galactic financial meltdown which means that they have to hold more money against riskier asset classes and SMEs are seen to be riskier asset classes. Therefore, it's more expensive and a bit trickier for banks as the reality is they were set up to lend to industrial revolution era companies. They've got regulation which they can say, quite rightly and quite honestly, is impeding their ability to lend to SMEs.

So, we thought 'Right, that's absolutely great, we'll get loads of referrals from banks.' No. We have had to go to the extreme lengths of getting an entirely new law through the Houses of Parliament to mandate banks to refer to non-banks. It's absolutely shocking that this is actually requiring legislation, but it is. It received Royal Assent in March 2015 which is just under a year and a half after we first took the idea to Number 10. It really does make David vs. Goliath look like a fair fight because we're so tiny and they've got hundreds of years of established practice and very deep pockets.

My advice and guidance is: don't be stupid. Understand the scale of the task you've decided to take on, but if you do then go through that phase of dawning realisation that it is actually a shockingly enormous task then you're going to have to be bloody minded, tenacious and you're going to have to get the rules changed to make it fairer. But the good news is that the industry is growing very fast. In 2012 a quarter of a billion pounds traded. In 2014 one and three quarter billion pounds traded.

This is through the sector.

Yes. That's the thing that matters, right? Because it's not just about GLI Finance's portfolio of SME alternative finance companies, it's actually about growing the sector. That's my other point of guidance which is: stop being so obsessed with yourself. Because somebody who is just obsessed with yourself, when you're trying to change something as fundamental as finance for half of our GDP, you can't just focus on your proposition, you've actually got to create something more.

I'm hearing fairness.

Yes, and I wouldn't overdo it. Fairness is important in all things, but just don't be naïve and assume that it's going to be fair. Understand that you may have to change the field of battle so that you have a fighting chance.

So, it is a lot easier to walk into the high street and establish a premium coffee brand. Why? Because premium coffee brands have been well established in this country for a decade or more. You expect to be able to walk into any high street and see a range of premium coffee brands. So, as much as it may look like a crowded market, we are trained, as consumers, to drink premium coffee.

SMEs expect to go to their bank and ask for money and they expect, actually, to be turned down. Then they expect not to do anything else. So, you're changing something gigantic in terms of how finance is delivered, but you're also educating. I did make a very bad joke, about five years ago, where I said "We're not in the business of alternative finance, we're in the business of education." Everybody laughed. All I can tell you is nobody's laughing anymore because it's so true and it's shocking how ill-informed SMEs are about options for financing their businesses.

What makes you so passionate?

Well, I don't think of it as passion. I'm sure if you saw me up on stage giving a speech about this kind of stuff then you would describe it as passion. I don't feel wildly emotional about it; I'm not a wildly emotional person.

Belief then...

Yes, it's a much more logical, rational characteristic, I think. If the numbers don't stack up, don't do it because you're just leading people into a battle they're never going to win and there's going to be nothing there if you do win. So, don't do that. Do the analysis, understand the opportunity and work out what you need to do to secure your fair share or, ideally, a bit more than your fair share of that opportunity.

You've got what, to many, would appear to be an insurmountable wall of industry and institution. Not only that, but having made inroads you've then got an enormous amount of educating to do. In the face of these huge challenges, if you were advising someone else, what would you say?

It really is the quality of resilience. So, I think it is stupidity, bloody mindedness and resilience. So, you have to be stupid, you have to not understand the scale of what it is that you're trying to take on and to not understand that you're going into a big boy's fight with toothpicks. They have got established armies of hundreds of thousands of people and an established infrastructure and established distribution network and they are the first port of call.

You have none of that. You have a smart way to get money to people who need it, as and when they need it. You absolutely have that, but they haven't heard of you. They've heard of RBS or Barclays or Lloyds. If you want to make a change this big, you have to fundamentally not understand the scale of what you're taking on otherwise you wouldn't do it. Sensible people would not do this. The dawning realisation comes upon you, you have to understand 'OK, it's a bigger fight than I was expecting.'

There's a huge business opportunity here for Britain's SMEs to get money as and when they need it to drive the growth in their business. That is a huge business opportunity. It's a huge business opportunity for them and it's a huge market opportunity for the businesses that solve that problem, which we can.

It's about smart technology and smart processes and smart underwriting and smart credit analysis. Then it's tenacity because the fight will take years. Years and years and years. In reality it may take decades or more. It's that fundamental a shift and you've got to be tenacious enough to say 'I'm not backing down, I'm raising more money, I'm doing this.' I think those really are the three overriding characteristics.

What mistakes would you advise others to avoid?

My main mistake was, as I say, stupidity, so do better on the understanding than I did. Recognise there may be unknown unknowns. There may be things that are so big you haven't spotted them yet. The scale of the problem was that I was standing with my nose pressed up against the Great Wall of China. I knew it was big, but I didn't know it was that big. The advice I would give is: better understand the challenge, but really, what you're really assessing, is not the size of the challenge, but whether or not you're up for it. So, understand yourself. Do you want to make your life difficult for a substantial period of time? Because that's what it's going to take. If you decide no, I'd rather have an easier life or run a lifestyle business or work for someone else, those are all absolutely legitimate choices. You don't have to put yourself through the challenge of creating a new industry, you really don't. Find something else.

In summary then, the advice you gave was around understanding the challenge and trying to find out what you don't know. There'll be things that you didn't realise you were unaware of.

Try and get people to identify the great big blind spots that you've been happily ignoring. It does mean going and talking to people and listening to what they say. They may not be right and you may not want to hear what they're saying. That's also fine, but at least go and listen and don't be put off. Really, don't be put off.

Have you got an example of where you have been tenacious to achieve an outcome?

It really is this alternative finance industry. Realising that actually, in order to create the economic opportunity for our country, you had to get legislation passed. We're not through that battle yet. The Royal Assent came through at the end of March. We've then got a further nine months of getting the secondary legislation in place and the banks complying. It's not going to be easy.

You seem to be a woman who confronts the challenges head on.

Yes, not always a smart thing to do, but I tend to think, if you wanted to go and work with the banks on something like this, then (1) they don't feel that they need to work with you and (2) their business model is broken so you can't incrementally improve the situation and make a difference, it has to be a fundamental shift.

So, you will tend to find pioneers in any walk of life. Bloody minded, tenacious – those are all pioneering characteristics. Stupid, that's definitely a pioneering characteristic. The people who will path-find in a new industry or a new service or a new product will tend to be the people who don't listen when people say 'Why don't you just go home and do something that is a little bit easier?' They tend not to be the people who do that and behave in that way. You don't want too many of these people around because they're a nuisance. You will not find a huge number of this characteristic type around because they'd drive us all nuts. I drive myself nuts. I'm sure I drive other people nuts at times too.

But there are other characteristics that you bring in at different phases in the cycle. So, there are the people who are operators of businesses. They run things, they incrementally improve. Those are valuable skills as well. It's just you don't tend to find them at the pioneering, painful end of the pointy bit.

If you were getting on a plane and had 30 seconds, what one more piece of advice would you give?

Choose who you listen to. Everybody will have an opinion and you have to know your own mind well enough as to who you should listen to because there are lots and lots and lots of people out there who would like you to do something which is in their interest, not yours, and not in the greater interest, not to achieve the bigger goal. So, choose who you listen. Listen to everyone, consult wisely, but choose who you really listen to.

What's enabled you to choose the right people to listen to?

Gut instinct and a good understanding of what people are really like.

Thank you so very much and keep pioneering on behalf of our SMEs.

Thank you.

In brief

If you want to be a pioneer of change you need to be tenacious, resilient, bloody minded and a little stupid.

With any ground-breaking new idea, find out what you don't know from those who have been through something similar. Ask others, but choose who you decide to listen to.

Try to get to grips with the unknown unknowns. Get as clear a picture as you can of exactly what you're getting into and decide up-front if it's really for you. Deciding that it isn't is a perfectly legitimate choice.

Alan Ridealgh: "Be true to yourself and people will follow"

Alan Ridealgh is MD of Muntons, a company which produces around 180,000 tonnes of malt each year, enough to fill over ninety Olympic sized swimming pools, using barley mainly grown within a fifty mile radius of their maltings at Stowmarket in Suffolk.

The malt produced is used to supply the brewing and distilling industries and to make a wide range of ingredients such as malt extract, malt flour and flakes and homebrew kits.

They supply these products to over sixty countries worldwide through a network of agents and distributors and through their own US company and Asian office.

Muntons ingredients are used extensively in products that we consume every day. Malt is used in beer and whiskey, but less obviously in vinegar, bread, breakfast cereals, confectionery and convenience meals to name a few. Muntons supply customers such as Carlsberg, Weetabix and Wilkinson's. Ever wondered where the malt in Malteasers comes from?

Thank you taking part in this project and helping to inspire business owners everywhere. Having met you a few times, I have been struck by how compelling you are as a leader. I come away with the sense that you have a certain air that positively influences people to want to follow you hence I was keen to talk further and understand that more.

Before that, what are the highlights of your story to this point?

Well, I started with the business at our Yorkshire Maltings in 1980 which is a staggering 35 years ago. With a degree in Zoology at the University of Newcastle I had a couple of years working for the Ministry of Agriculture as a Scientific Officer and started work with Muntons. I spent two years as a trainee grain buyer – became a trainee farm manager during that period too, as the business owned quite a large animal farm – and then I moved to Stowmarket as a grain buyer. I stayed at Stowmarket for five years and then moved back to Bridlington, again on the grain side, but during that period we became quite aggressive in buying other businesses. I was involved in acquiring and then running a number of grain businesses: one in Yorkshire, one in Suffolk, one in Scotland, a seed business in Suffolk (cereal seeds these were), a pet food business, and ran the haulage business and several other bits and pieces.

How many of these were you running at a time?

I think I was MD of five or six companies during that period, as well as running the grain operation. I then moved to Stowmarket again and several years after that I amalgamated those into one operation which we call Muntons Grain which made it much more manageable. I happily ran that until about 2000, when we reviewed what we wanted to do as a business and, really, we decided we would focus on a core competency of making stuff and selling that to customers as an ingredient, whether it was for brewing, distilling or into the food industry.

The other parts of the business were a distraction, but some of them were very valuable to us, so over a little space of time it was a question of saying 'What do we want to keep? What do we not want to keep?' and from there we essentially closed down or sold (generally we sold) all of those businesses and slimmed down to just doing the core job, but we did retain some of the important things to us from those businesses which essentially were the reasons that we got involved with them in the first place.

You really played to the core strengths of the business.

Yes, and really we've kept with that since then. And I ended up running the malt and grain business and then in 2005 the existing MD here became unwell and I was made deputy MD. In 2006 the job was advertised through head hunters. I applied for it and got the job. It wasn't an automatic selection and it wasn't a job that I ever wanted to do. I was more than happy doing what I was doing with the grain background. I had that love of agriculture and grain so I was really at a point where I was more than happy with that, but when the job became available and I wasn't automatically put into the pot I was slightly annoyed, but in hindsight it was absolutely the right decision.

So, that really gave me the incentive to say 'I'd like to do that job, but why would I like to do that job?' Well, the reason I wanted to do the job and the conclusion I came to was that I wanted to preserve the things that I felt were important about Muntons, that somebody else coming in from outside might accidently remove or destroy. That was the incentive I really needed to try and get that job and I don't think that I have ever prepared as much in my life as I did for the series of interviews with the head hunters and eventually with the shareholders. The process made me passionate about wanting to do the job.

It's interesting, isn't it? As you say, you didn't think that it was something that you wanted to do, but that passion for maintaining the values of the business that were so important to you really contributed to your desire for the role.

Yes, absolutely, and I suppose it was because I'd been here quite a long time at that point and I really liked the people around me meant I didn't really want to lose that.

After three interviews the hard work paid off and I got the job. For me, it was good that I wasn't automatically promoted. I had to go through the selection process the same as anybody else, so there was no 'He's only got the job because he's worked here for 20 years' from other staff members.

It sounds hard earned.

Yes, but I think it was right.

And it made you want that job.

Yes, and it's something that I've used with a couple of my colleagues when vacancies have arisen and they've not thanked me at the time, but they certainly have afterwards when they've been promoted.

When I got the job we were pretty much at a low as a business although we'd been investing quite heavily in plant and machinery. I therefore had the benefit of having some good equipment and products available to me and quite quickly was able to tailor those to specific customers which set us on quite a strong upward trend.

It's great to see how quickly the company has expanded.

Yes, we certainly did grow and expand quickly. We decided to concentrate on core activities back in 2000 at a time when we were under pressure from the commodity markets. The grain markets were also extremely volatile during the same period and that had a huge effect on our business in terms of cash, particularly when you're spending twice as much on raw materials in one year as you did in the previous year. It's tough. There were certain customers out there in our brewing areas that didn't value us and they were possibly, in total, half of our malting trade.

So, we decided that we weren't going to sell to them anymore and we would find another way of finding customers that valued us. As a result, our profitability dipped one year because that was the year of transition, but we were always confident that we'd come through it quite strongly and we came through it the following year as we successfully made that transition with a near record profit, followed by a record profit.

We had completely changed our outlook. Instead of supplying to the commodity customers we were supplying more bespoke products at higher margin and that's worked for us ever since then. What's been really nice about it is that we also found some of the customers we thought we were going to walk away wouldn't let us go.

That was a surprise, a very pleasant surprise because we'd always based our business on quality and service. Being a smaller producer we needed to be better than everybody else and then to find that two very big global brewers would not let us get away from them, by that I mean they paid us higher margin. In fact with one of them now we're almost back to where we were before we took this route and are nearly their biggest European supplier.

They valued your values.

Yes, and that was a little bit of a surprise to us. I think because there were other alternatives, they could've decided to go to other people, but they didn't and part of that was our sustainability, which was the bigger picture, and our efforts and passion about sustainability. Sustainability was part of their growth strategy as well and nobody else was doing it in our industry.

In those times there must've been the worry of 'Am I doing the right thing and is this going to work?' It's very courageous.

Yes, people have said it's very brave and I always read brave as meaning stupid because sometimes it is. It's very easy to continue doing the same thing, but something's always stuck in my mind; if you continue doing the same thing in the same way you'll end up with the same result. We had to change the game, we had to do something. It just was not sustainable in any way whatsoever.

And of course we briefed the shareholders, banks, staff, customers – everybody – and we kept them updated as we progressed. We advised our shareholders and banks that it could be bumpy for a year because unfortunately, at that time, our financial calendar and company calendar year didn't coincide, so the danger was that it went over two financial years. So, we set off by saying that at the financial year (the end of September) we will make a change, but we may not have got it completed until the end of the calendar year and that's exactly what happened in the end which meant that we dipped very slightly into the red in that year, but bounced back immediately from the start of the calendar year.

It wasn't easy because when you actually do go into the red people, they say 'but you've just lost money,' but this was explained to all concerned and that we expected to bounce back quite strongly. The banks were also questioning why we had lost money, to which we reminded them this was anticipated. The banks were also going through difficult periods at that time as well, but the good thing that came out of the situation was that they actually sat down with us and said 'Is there a better way of doing this with you?' Eventually we came to a fantastic deal with our banks for funding the business going forward, initially with RBS and Lloyds and now just with RBS. This takes away all of the stress and worry we were having about the commodity markets using asset-based lending. Our stock is the thing that varies in price so it just took it all out of the way. We work very closely with our banks and have an extremely good and strong relationship with them, and they designed this product specifically for us which is quite flattering really.

It's interesting that we're going right back where we started our conversation, with openness and trust, shared values and collaboration.

Yes, and I think getting that across as well builds quite a lot of confidence between different people. It's interesting that values and vision come together really, don't they? Organisations do surveys to see how you get your message through to staff and we took part in one of these. One of the questions in there was "Do you understand and share the companies values and vision?" and we got something like 86% that said absolutely, some said not sure and there were a couple of no's, but of course you've got new people coming in all the time. The funny thing is though, we'd never ever communicated our values and visions.

It was through actions?

Yes.

And living them.

Yes, and that made me think let's try and make sure that we do articulate what our values and visions are, so that those new people coming through and those that may have forgotten them all have the same awareness. Now that the business has spread worldwide, we need to make sure that our values and vision are consistent in each area of the world that we operate in. This is a big challenge currently as we're building a new factory in Thailand.

Congratulations!

Yes, it's quite exciting really.

During your journey, have you ever been frustrated by a repeating pattern, an obstacle that kept coming up? Did something you learned about yourself help you overcome that obstacle?

I'll refer back to what I said earlier. If you keep doing something in the same way you'll only get the same result. We had to say to ourselves 'How do we break those loops?'

There was nowhere in our industry where those loops were being broken so it wasn't as if there was something there to copy. I'm quite happy to copy things if they're successful, but there was nothing there.

At the same time, on sustainability there was nothing there from anybody else so we really had to talk through as an executive team how we viewed this. Did we think we could do these things? We were certain that we could lead on sustainability because we are passionate about it. We also believe that we have a responsibility in terms of sustainability to the community and to the environment, but also to our shareholders. In other words, we've got to be financially viable going forward as well.

It works. It's a way of thinking. It doesn't cost us any money, it actually makes us money and it's absolutely brilliant. I cannot understand why businesses don't grasp it with both hands rather than seeing it as an obstacle. I've heard somebody describe it as a "paying lip service to" just this week. You actually lead with it and in return it delivers for you in lots and lots of ways.

And that was shared vision and values.

It was a review of it. We had to carry our shareholders with us, who were very sceptical about it, but we've moved it on considerably now. It was similar with the decision we made to stop doing business in the same way and breaking the loop.

Among those personal light bulb moments, you mentioned not being able to continue doing business in the same way and being very passionate about that. Is there anything else, perhaps about yourself, that you learnt in that journey too?

During that journey there were some difficulties. Not everybody came with us and we did have some changes within the business, at director level as well, but there was a huge amount of support and that really surprised me. You always hope you've got support, but there are times at which it's really there and it's charitable. People are lining up with you and that was really needed to get us through quite a sticky period that we went through two or three years ago and that support has continued.

That was the light bulb moment to me, that if we got that support we could do anything. There was another light bulb moment which came more recently a couple of years ago, when we'd gone through some of these changes with the commodity customers and we were working with our bespoke customers. We realised just how important we were to these customers, not in a moment getting complacent or cocky with it, but 'we have a place here' and that gave us a lot of confidence to say we can get a margin out of this business and that has come, that has worked.

What do you believe it is about you that really has gained that level of trust and support?

Passion, I think. Commitment to the business, and honesty and openness. I can't lie because I can never remember if I lie so there's no point in doing it. People may at times think I'm a bit blunt, but hopefully not in an unpleasant way. I just can't do the untruth bit so I tend to share with everybody.

That openness and authenticity, being yourself and recognising that you bring people with you, but not getting cocky about it or using it other than for common good, are fabulous traits.

If you were hopping on a plane and had 30 seconds, what one more bit of advice would you give?

Be yourself. It would just be to be yourself.

Can I add a suggestion?

Yes.

And be true to yourself.

Yes, oh absolutely. I think I've written down here, value your values.

Thank you very much for your time. I'm sure there are going to be a lot of people that will be inspired by reading about your journey.

My pleasure. I've really enjoyed talking to you, Angela.

In brief

Play to the core strengths of your business. Carry out a review to ensure that you are focusing on the right areas. Dispose of any areas that are distracting or not profitable. If they have any value, sell them.

Find customers that value you as a business. This will enable you to supply bespoke products at a higher margin. You may be surprised to find that some customers who you expected to leave behind may not be willing to let you go!

If you do the same thing the same way, you'll get the same result. Think of innovative ways to break the loop and change the game and you will see results. Be passionate about sustainability. If you lead with sustainability it will, in turn, deliver for you in lots and lots of ways. Can you afford not to?

Work closely with your banks and, if you can, build up effective relationships with them. This will help relieve the stresses and worries of the everyday business world and they could even design specialist products tailored to your business needs.

Values and vision really come together and build a lot of confidence between different people. Ensure that they are known through the organisation.

If you have the right support you can do anything you want to.

Realise how important you are to your customers, but don't get complacent. Know your place within the market and that will grow your confidence as an organisation.

Lastly, always remember to be yourself and true to your values – it will take you a long way!

Muntons Ingredients manufacture a comprehensive range of grain malts and further process these into a range of malted ingredients for food producers, bakers and confectioners to add flavour, colour and texture to their products.

Our malted products are endless and can all be found on our website at www.muntons.co.uk. We're so proud of them that we've produced our own Consumer Recipe Booklet which can be downloaded for free on our website.

Russ Stilwell: "Live your values"

Russell Stillwell's story is unique in this collection; he started out in his chosen career path early. He began his apprenticeship to train as an electrician following his work experience at school, aged 14 (albeit he completed his GCSEs). He found his pathway from a young age and stuck to it by being given an amazing opportunity and start in life by his then boss and family friend, Cliff Longman.

Russell qualified, worked hard and progressed to qualification as an electrician aged 19. He decided to start finding his own private work, opening doors of opportunity through word of mouth and leading to the establishment of a private client base. This client base would eventually form the basis for Russell starting his first business, RS Electrical Contractor Ltd.

Initially, although only providing electrical services, Russell's customers liked the way he operated so much that he got regular requests to find other services that offered the same high quality results. Over the years, Russell has put together a team of experts and now has a strong in-house team offering:

- electrical services

- mechanical services
- energy efficiency
- design and management

The team are dedicated to providing solutions within the construction and facilities management industry that deliver a combination of excellence and value. They hold themselves accountable for working to high professional and personal standards whilst always looking to raise the bar.

Hi, Russ. Can you tell us a bit more about your journey and that of the business, particularly around the personal growth that enabled you to get to where you are today.

My journey starts from the age of 14, having done work experience with a local company called Longman Electrical Contractors. I was not engaged at school and was only passionate about certain lessons with a lacking in career direction. Having been given two weeks' work experience at Ilford swimming pool, it was my intention to bunk off my work experience. One day I made this clear to a great man called Cliff Longman (dad to a close school friend) - the rest was history!

So, Cliff Longman gave me two weeks' work experience on some domestic rewires and within that time I remember learning what appeared to be so much in a short space of time. At the end of it I wasn't expecting any money. At the time I did a milk round and got about £8 for a Saturday morning's work. I received unexpected payment at the end of the two weeks. I got £100. This changed my view on life; money for doing something I loved for someone I really respected and looked up to. A decision was made very quickly. That was what I wanted to do – I wanted to be an electrician and nothing was going to stop me. I could've been good at school if I applied myself, but having had such a compelling work experience both inspired and helped me from a young age to find a career path, combining practical development with a subject that I wanted to learn. So, Cliff took me under his wing and I started a very, very early apprenticeship at the age of 14 as well as officially still being at school.

When I came to leave school and was already one and a half years into what I was going to be doing, we then got to the stage where we had to set up my day release at college. So, I worked four days and went to college one day. I did that with Longman Electrical Contractors and completed what was my electrical apprenticeship.

You must have been very young to have that qualification.

I was quite young, I was 19. I remember being young and thinking 'I can do this,' but was also quite apprehensive of having responsibility. At 21 I was looking after small sites with the responsibility of delivering the work and had apprentices working under me. In those days Cliff was very much a role model to me so I looked up to him; his ways were my ways. I very much overhauled my demeanour, my personality. He brought me out of me. That set very strong foundations for where I am today.

Cliff saw something very special in you.

I think so, but when you're young you make the mistake of wanting things too quickly and you suddenly find out through talking to friends and going down the pub what you could earn, and I actually made the big mistake of letting that get into my head. At the age of 20 I spread my wings and said to Cliff that I'd been offered something else and I wanted to go. I think there was disappointment there from both him and his brother Keith's perspective, but I had made my mind up to go and do it. I think they knew I would always be back; they weren't wrong! I can remember a 'talk' from him about having to go and spread my wings, but to remember that the door is always open. I got a taster of how tough the world can be.

I went and worked for a company who were doing a big estate in Barking and, because I'd been running sites for a couple of years then, I was given the responsibility of looking after the electrical installations on that site. At 21 I had guys working under me who were 40 years old plus. I suppose I did well. I delivered the work and I delivered it with the passion and integrity that I was always taught to deliver with, but I was inexperienced and games were played within the company I was working with. I soon then realised 'better the devil you know than the devil you don't' and I went back to Longmans. I had a year and a half away before I went back there. I suppose in doing that, it then developed me as it should have done, becoming more streetwise. I then worked on some bigger commercial projects, really getting the chance to fly at the work I was doing and get on in life earning good money as a sub-contractor in price work.

So, that was all going well until a time when, whilst working on a site in Tonbridge, I tripped up a set of stairs and unfortunately, as there wasn't a temporary stair rail, I fell through the stairs and landed two landings below straight on my coccyx. So, I was then in hospital for a period and had damaged all the soft tissues in the base of my spine. Luckily I didn't break it. When I'd gone back to Cliff I was self-employed so it was a bit stressful not earning whilst I was ill. At the same time in my personal life I had a break-up with my partner so I decided to go away and take some time out and went to Cyprus for six months running a bar which developed a really strong following. Doing everything for myself, with very little money for that period really grounded me.

What happened after Cyprus?

I then came home and went back to working with Cliff straight away, but it was different. I was different. I wasn't the same person and things had changed at LEC. I wasn't stimulated with my safe career path as I learned to live on hardly any money in Cyprus and found out that passion could make good things happen, as it did with the bar I was working in over there. I made my mind up and took the decision to start getting my own work which started with me doing a little bit of call-out work for a conservatory company as well as furnishing existing clients, friends and family. I opened a sole trader account as RS Electrical and the order book started to grow.

When was that, roughly?

That would have been 2003.

And that was the birth of what is now RSE Building Services...

Yes, I suppose so. I didn't think that at the time. I just thought it would be a side-line and that I'd get a little bit of work. I was hopelessly naïve then, Angela. I didn't know what Excel was and I didn't have a laptop. I just about had a cash card, I didn't even have a debit card. Everything was dealt in cash and I was very basic in the way that I did things. So, I was still working for Cliff when I met my wife Deb as well as doing private work. I then had a difficult situation; a subsidiary company of one of the companies that Longman Electrical Contractors used to work for offered me work direct. I immediately thought that I couldn't do it because of the conflict with Cliff's company. However, this guy went out of his way to prove that the work wasn't connected and that he had a lot of work that he wanted to offer me personally. So, I went with it and took the decision to start taking that work on. I was up-front with Cliff and Longmans in telling them what I'd done, but it didn't go down very well at all.

It sounds like alarms bells were ringing from the outset and that, although you were up-front about it, things weren't as they seemed.

The work was great and there was loads of it, but it was the relationship side and what I started to feel. I was starting to feel quite guilty. However, with the new work the business really grew. I was doing three or four re-wires a week and I'd taken one apprentice on to assist with the conservatory work. Working long hours and trying to do it all myself, with the excellent support of Deb. One of the builders who I was working with did all of the refurbishment work on hotels in London and he wanted me to start doing work for him as well. He saw what I did, how I did it and how thorough we were and he wanted me to start working in the Berkeley and Westbury Hotels. So, I started doing little bits in both hotels with him until such time that we got offered a very big contract which was the renewal of sub mains in the Berkeley Hotel. At the same time as that was happening, there was 240 rooms to be refurbished in the Westbury hotel. Things were definitely on the up!

It was suddenly very big and it was very daunting. I had Sev who still works for me now. I felt confident that I could deliver, albeit this was nothing like I'd ever taken on before. It shows how naïve in business I really was. I was purely an electrician that had just started his own little company and grew something. I took on both those contracts and delivered them without even a care in the world or thought in the world for limiting my risks. I did them as a sole trader and that year I turned over £470,000. If anything had gone wrong I would have been totally personally liable. Looking back at that I can't believe what I was thinking, but I wasn't thinking, just letting passion and excitement lead the way; that's the reality of it. Our accountants at the time advised us in 2005 to becoming a limited company. Maybe I should've realised this earlier as we were taking extreme risks turning over so much money as a sole trader. Once realising this for myself we changed over to a limited company in 2005/6 and at that time we were doing work for new-build developers and local authorities. It grew very, very quickly, in a very short space of time.

Earlier you talked about your passion, integrity and the personal side. It sounds like those things were instrumental in your ability to deliver and build trusting relationships.

I think so. As it went on, one of the things that became recognisable was that my ability was what started it, but it wasn't my business acumen that got us to where we are today, it was purely passion and personality. We moved and came to Billericay from Wanstead and after realising that we didn't have the room within our (growing) family home to accommodate the business, we decided to take a lease on our first premises in Laindon.

What sort of turnover were you making then?

When we took that lease on we were turning over £750,000 in 2007. We actually decided to take it in April 2007 and that was a committal of £15,000 a year for five years under a full repairing lease.

That was a big step. What was the point when you thought 'right, OK, we're doing this?'

We'd been thinking about it for a while and there was a belief that the way the work was coming through the door at the time, we could do something and the business had the ability to go somewhere. I was young, there was money in the bank, we were getting paid regularly and were making sustainable profit margins. It was seen as an investment I suppose. We thought, we've come this far, let's go for it.

We then started to try and look for managers and get people to assist in the office. My management inexperience in running a business started to come through and recruiting was difficult. I remember us going in there and refurbishing the office. The work was still coming in, but Lehman Brothers went down, then NatWest, and the recession was plastered all over the news. We'd just used up all of our reserves to get the place to look how we needed it to. I'd made a big pension contribution that I regretted and by the September of that year I was fighting a battle to survive and it was a big one as well.

We then took on a big Council contract and that was a £1 million contract. We took the decision to nurture one egg and just focus on that purely. Still, a significant thing happened that would have a lasting impact on the business. A young lady joined our company called Elouise Eagling (who is now operations manager for the business) as an admin assistant. Her manager then left and I remember a conversation between myself and Elouise where I'm saying to her "Are you able to do this? Do you understand it?" To be fair to her, she was 19 then and she just grabbed it with both hands and ran with it. But being thrown in the deep end enabled Elouise to thrive and grow.

Then we got hit hard with a company going bust on us. Losing £150,000 was a real test on business survival. We still had work and we still had a great team so we ploughed on. The quality was out there from a work perspective, but we were struggling to pay suppliers. However, communication and honesty was the way forward.

Do you remember any light bulb moments following such a hard lesson?

The business went backwards slightly. I had to make people redundant and then pick it all up myself. Things were very tight; we had to ask the guys to take a pay cut. There were some significant things we had to do then to make things work, including getting rid of our existing accountants and taking on a new accountant who, without a doubt, made a difference, in me and the way we were doing things in the business. The best thing I did with this situation hanging over my company was communicate honestly and clearly to our employees and supply chain whilst maintaining what had to be a flawless service to our clients.

What would you say was the key learning for you?

My old accountants were just accountants. They gave little business advice and I decided to seek a practice offering business growth attributes. Our then new accountant, Richard Tufnell, could see what we were capable of and demonstrated a level of understanding and passion towards us that blew the previous ones away. He taught me how to do business. He came to see me each week with the accounts and I focused on getting the work done. Then we started to come out the other side. We had the ability from within the business to deliver. I'd grown in ability and skill-set without knowing or realising the extent. We had a brand that our clients bought simply because we delivered what we promised, on a broad spectrum and always to a high standard.

How were you different in terms of the industry standard?

I suppose the biggest thing was our attention to detail and finish; snag-less, pristine work. The smallest error would be picked up on, not only by me, but by the teams themselves as well. We then won a big project which was worth £1 million over a seven month timespan, installing a new generator set for a global commodity dealer. Now we were really going to be tested!

When was this?

We're at 2011/2. We had just delivered our first £1 million pound Mechanical and Electrical project successfully!

What was your turnover at that point?

£1.5-2 million. Then, just shortly after that in 2013, I engaged an expert in growing my skills in managing and leading the business.

What key areas of personal growth did you uncover?

I'm certainly calmer which is a good thing. I'm now in control, have good self-awareness and a greater awareness of other people as well. The tools that I've worked with and embraced for benefit in the business have been fundamental to me personally as well. When I think back to 2003, I'm now an improved person with additional skill sets. It's nice to get that feedback from people who know me well.

What specifics within you and the business do you see as key to the next phase?

Sustaining our high growth achieved last year of £5 million turnover, but ensuring the right profit is made. To look carefully at the business, with the learning point being that the most or biggest isn't always best. It's about quality, not quantity. I've always known that and I took for granted how good RSE's qualities were last year and assumed that they would be easily and quickly taught to and learned by new people coming into the business. This didn't work because values are learned by working and living within a culture over time. Expecting these to be embraced too quickly will result in a variance in values meaning a variance in quality and client satisfaction!

Recognising that when you want to grow your business, quality is what makes it viable for the long term. Also that beyond a certain size, quality cannot keep coming directly from you, but has to be delivered by others.

Yes. I think if you take me out of the equation you've just got a business that works and functions. I have a good team, a lot of risks get mitigated through my experiences over the years. You can't buy that and you can't just teach it, but I have to share as much as possible with the team so they can do even more for themselves.

If you had to share one aspect of your personal learning that you feel would benefit others, what would it be?

There are a few, but the first one that's been key to my growth is humility. From my favourite poem *If* by Rudyard Kipling, "If you can walk with kings, but never lose the common touch" – keep your feet firmly on the ground. If I hadn't have learnt to have done that, I don't think we'd be here today.

What would the second one be?

To ensure the company values are out there and known. Do all that you can to live them to the full yourself and ensure that your team live them the way you do too.

If you were hopping on a plane and had 30 seconds, what one more bit of advice would you share?

Love what you do and communicate clearly. Never forget life's journeys. Let that be the creator of your values so that it is those values that influence the culture of your thoughts and actions. Who you are being at any given moment in time will influence what you do and how you do it!

And what do you notice about what's going on around you?

Post-recession demand in the construction sector is so high that there is a shortage of available labour with the right skills. The new technology in 3D building information modelling (BIM) means that much more planning and risk management can be done up-front in the design of a building project. This reduces the time and cost downstream both in terms of manpower needed in the construction stage with fewer unforeseen risks coming to fruition.

With BIM, you can then also model how the finished building will operate and plan up-front for efficiencies to reduce the ongoing running and maintenance costs of the building once complete. The face of UK construction is changing in line with what's already in place in other countries such as America. RSE Building Services are leaders in this new world and we've already invested in the essential technology and development to achieve this. You need to keep ahead of the majority and be flexible.

So, don't get complacent and know what's happening in your market place...

Yes, exactly.

Thank you very much, Russ.

In brief

Set strong foundations for where you want your business to go, but don't make the mistake of wanting too much too soon; good things come to those who wait. When you start out in business, the world can be a very tough place and sometimes even the best of opportunities aren't as good as they seem. Sometimes it's better the devil you know than the devil you don't.

If you start out as a sole trader be careful of your liabilities if things go wrong. Mistakes on big jobs could be very costly and you could lose the roof over your own head so get a good accountant who will advise you properly on the correct decisions for you and your business.

Even when you least expect it the economy can cause you major problems. Be careful of your reserves and be sure to have enough for a rainy day because sometimes you have to go backwards to go forwards in the long term.

It is vital to grow your own skills in managing and leading the business. If you can, try and enlist the help of an expert to do this, who can equip you with the right tools to do it effectively. This will enable you to share as much as you can with your team and enable them to flourish, allowing you to move from managing to leading. You have to let go to let the business grow.

The company values are vital and it is important that they are shared freely amongst all staff members so that everybody can embrace and live them. This will ensure that all customers get the very best service possible. Remember that quality is much more important than quantity and will enable you to leave every job with a satisfied customer ready to give you more work and recommend you to others.

Always pay attention to what you're doing. Look hard at what's going on around you, what's going on in your mind and your values every day to make sure that it's all aligned. Don't get complacent; keep up with what's happening in your market place.

Angus Thirlwell: "If you want a sustainable, profitable business, get a bit of brand WOW!"

The very first Hotel Chocolat shop opened its doors to guests in North London in 2004. It was the start of a pioneering revolution in British chocolate.

Since that Watford shop opened ten years ago, another 75 Hotel Chocolat boutiques have opened in the UK.

Hotel Chocolat is the creation of British entrepreneurs Angus Thirlwell and Peter Harris. Everything they do is guided by three basic values, and always will be:

1. Originality: Being fresh, creative and innovative, and always one surprising step ahead.

2. Authenticity: Keeping it real. Growing their own cocoa beans on their beautiful plantation in St. Lucia, creating their own chocolate recipes and even making chocolate fresh from the bean in their cocoa bar-cafes.

3. Ethics: Reconnecting their love of chocolate with its roots. They believe that cocoa farmers worldwide deserve respect and a fair deal. And that's what they strive to offer, from Saint Lucia to Ghana where they pay their growers above market value to give a fair deal all round.

In the following interview, I met Angus Thirlwell at Rabot 1745, a relatively new addition to the Hotel Chocolat family, bringing the cocoa-inspired cuisine of the flagship Hotel Chocolat Hotel in St. Lucia to the UK.

Named after the company's cocoa plantation in St. Lucia, Rabot 1745 has the feel of a plantation house transported into the heart of London's vibrant Borough Market.

Hi Angus. Many thanks indeed for being part of this special book to share the learning of successful founding entrepreneurs with those earlier on in their entrepreneurial journey. So, where did your business learning begin?

I went on the Cranfield Business Growth Programme and I can remember a time when the business felt like it was on the cusp of something and I didn't want us to mess it up. We had made a few mistakes, but we were at the point where the chocolate tasting club (our monthly subscription scheme) was really about to take off and I had a sense that I had to make sure that I was as well-equipped as I possibly could be to lead us to the next level.

The big thing that I got out of the business growth programme is that I shouldn't feel bad about not being busy all the time. It's better to be thinking, planning and strategising about what's around the corner, rather than just going home every day exhausted in a blood and guts role, feeling that unless I'm in the middle of everything I'm not worthy of being the leader of the business.

So, that learning to get out of the doing has really helped me get to where I am now and I appreciate that some people want to feel that people are dependent upon them, be the one with all the answers and the hero in the middle of the business. I also see that sometimes with new employees, where people don't want to allow anybody else to be developing, they want to be at the centre of it and have everybody else dependent upon them. It's not sustainable and is driven by insecurity and, ultimately, is selfish because they're not putting the needs of the business before their own.

So, I think that was a really important lesson for me to learn. It had a very positive impact on the growth of the business. Whether I would have got there myself without going on the business growth programme, I don't know. I think I probably would have, but it might have taken longer and with more mistakes.

Sometimes I describe it to business owners as continually making yourself redundant from the things that you are 'doing' now in order to let others move up and take them on. The business growth comes from you moving further and further into leading and out of doing.

Yes, and in our business there is a slightly different dynamic because I still own the business 50/50 with my business partner and we still work actively within the business. However, our relationship has changed in terms of executive responsibilities over that time.

When we first started out I was joint managing director with Peter Harris, my business partner, and I was very happy about that. He is about eight years older than I am and already had a couple of business start-ups under his belt. I just knew that I didn't want to be junior to him and our relationship wasn't like that.

But over time it changed further and I wanted to be the leader in terms of executive responsibilities. I was very happy to have Peter as a shareholder on equal status with me, but in terms of leading the business and driving the brand forward I had to be the one. So, we managed to do that without falling out, which is good, but part of the benefit of the business programme that I completed was also to seek confidence in my own strategic ideas.

Many put off conversations like that, for fear of rocking the boat. How did you approach that initial discussion with Peter?

Respectfully and separating the issues and the opportunities of shareholding and ownership from those of executive responsibilities or directorship. I think that provides you with a fantastic structure for this type of conversation. Saying that I don't want to change anything on a shareholder level, we want the business to go from here to here, my thoughts are that we should do it this way and then having a good discussion about it. We agreed that we would try it for a while and see how it went, and it worked very well so we kept it that way.

So, on the one hand we have management capability, the logical, rational, process and structural side of business, and on the other, leadership capability - being a visionary, building a strong sustainable brand and culture – the behavioural side of the business, inspiring people to get on board. And understanding that the business needs both to really thrive.

What's been your biggest personal learning on the leadership side of that journey?

Trying to search for the simplest thing all the time. Subtle messages don't work very well. Subtle messages are OK when you've got a very tight group of people who are fellow addicts of the business with the same view as you have. Taking it outside of that group is hard; you end up with different interpretations. So, simplicity is the key: working at that message, keep refining it down and then go back and refining it again. Whenever I've forced myself to do that, I've never regretted it. Yet, whenever I've gone too quickly out of the starting gates with something and got very excited about it, trying to tell people without refining it in my own mind and in my own communication, it's ultimately been frustrating because they don't get it quickly enough and they don't understand it, so we go around again. So, that's one of the biggest things around my learning.

That's really pertinent as I work a lot with growing businesses around distilling their brand and the values that make them unique into a few simple statements. I noticed that yours were distilled into three clear statements and I love the fact that there are only three. It's nice and easy to remember, but all-pervasive too.

Three always works, doesn't it? Whenever I do speeches, it's always three. I can only remember three things at a time. Since then I've read lots of books and come back to three's a great number to base any strategy around and then you can break each one up into smaller parts of course.

How has that simplicity of message been key in your business journey?

Our business history is really 25 years. So, I started with this 25 years ago and we evolved gradually into Hotel Chocolat. We divide our business history into 15 years of apprenticeship, lots of knockbacks and trying to build lots of different models. Some worked quite quickly, other ones it took me ten years to get to work, like our internet chocolate business.

You were a very early adopter of selling online.

I should've probably given up before I did!

The problem with selling chocolate by internet or mail order is that it's actually a low ticket item so it means that you never quite have enough marketing budget to be able to compete with fashion retailers or big brands.

The challenge is how you become an aspirational, luxury brand with very little marketing budget when you're trying to build a database and you haven't got a lot to invest and acquire each buyer. That's a very difficult thing to round off, but the good news is that once you've got there, there are very few people who can follow you.

So, the drive was that once we can achieve this it will be a great place because internet chocolate retailing is hard. And it took us a full ten years to get it working, probably a full five years to get it going and then five years to really refine it.

What sort of loops did you work through before you knew that the business had started to fly?

Underneath the hood of Hotel Chocolat we are several different business models and I think a lot of brand-led businesses have to overcome this issue of being masters of several themes.

One of the things I realised I had to do to make the internet chocolate business work is actually become an expert at online marketing, so I went on lots of courses and read lots of books, even though we had a couple of marketing people at that point. I knew more about it than they did.

I then tried to use their skills in line with mine to fast-track it to a model that worked. Once I'd found the formula I could let the reins go a bit further, but the most I could expect from competent marketers was to maintain the status quo. There would be no seismic shift in the business model and yet we did need to shift it to get to the point where it was worth investing more in. So, step by step, I think it's good to become an expert in different fields and not just be a one trick pony.

I've had to learn about retailing in terms of the shop-keeper skills, the design of physical spaces, things like café models, restaurant models, agriculture, mixing properties of cocoa. Fortunately I'm really interested in these things so it's not a hardship at all, but I think there are so many things that you need to know being a brand-led business – it comes with the challenge.

That willingness to learn and to really get into the detail to fully understand it. How did you keep faith that you were on the right track?

It was never an issue. We've certainly closed quite a few businesses, so we're not averse to reading the messages. For example, we had a period where we supplied supermarkets with their own label chocolates and the appeal of that was a short-term way to get extra capital into the business.

We know how to create ranges and do exciting things with chocolate and so, very quickly, I was doing most of the chocolates for the two most premium supermarkets. We had two to three years of raking in some decent profits from that, but pretty soon it became apparent that it was leading nowhere, which we fully expected, but how quickly it went from being quite good into being something that we needed to get out of was quite startling.

What sort of timescale are we talking about?

About three years. So, we went from doing nothing, to doing a couple of million pounds and making decent profit again, but ultimately it was distracting. The motives of the supermarkets weren't straightforward and all the effort wasn't actually building anything cumulative in terms of a sustainable brand of our own. All the efforts you've gone to leave no trace of you, so that's desperately unappealing.

So, how did we keep the faith? Well, when we created Hotel Chocolat, I was very clear that this is a brand-led business, the brand stands for something, and that then gave me a lot more to defend and I suppose seek strength from. As soon as you're a brand that means something it becomes alive, rather than just making a few boxes of chocolates every day and then going home.

We managed to turn it around so that it meant something to other people and I can see the light go on in their eyes, and even in years where we weren't making much money, I could take reassurance in the fact that we were building a brand that was actually heading somewhere and we were building it for the long term.

When I look at companies like Thornton's, I think one of the reasons that we're beating them is because they run the business for the short-term. We think that long-term planning will win out. I've never wavered, Peter's never wavered, we've always believed in strategy and fortunately had enough success so that it never was a question. We've certainly had adversity, but nothing that's ever seriously made us question what we were doing.

In terms of your customer base and seeing them connect with the brand, when did you get to a tipping point where it just seemed to take on a life of its own?

Ah, yes, it was a clearly discernible tipping point actually. The first when we had our previous brand before Hotel Chocolat. It was a delivered, internet-based, chocolate business called ChocExpress. It described what it did on the tin, but no more, and yet our product was very good. So, we had a reasonable degree of success with that and people would say "I've had some of your chocolates recently, and they were surprisingly nice." "'Surprisingly' – why?" I wanted to ask. I started thinking that this brand name isn't right for us anymore and we needed an extra dimension.

I had come to understand that chocolate has a very strong emotional value and although we were delivering a very good product in terms of functional value, we weren't really delivering emotional value. So, how could we do that? I then started thinking about a brand which would bring another dimension of escapism. I took advice from people I respected, especially in the internet mail order field, and said that I was thinking about changing the brand name, and most said don't do it, what you've got works really well here, stick with your knitting because if you change the brand name, your customers might not like it.

I suppose their view was that I was 80% towards where I wanted to get, why risk it for another 20%? I suppose I hadn't articulated very well that I wanted to go further, so I ignored the advice and created the brand name Hotel Chocolat. It was very successful. We got a bit of a lift from our existing customers who were the most important ones, so we managed to gradually bring them on board, track their buying habits and knew that the re-brand had given us a lift there.

The next thing was to see if it was better at enticing new customers in and that was where it was resoundingly better. I can remember that feeling of getting wind in the sails. When people start liking and talking about your brand on social media and knowing that we never had that with ChocExpress, wow, this is really the power of a good brand. But it's more than a name plate or a letter head or some smart packaging; it's got to mean something and you've got to stick by it. Being clear about our responsibility in terms of our behaviour, the things we don't do, the things that we do to protect and nurture that brand, and it's definitely been the best move we've ever made.

How do you explicitly maintain that?

The brand values of Originality, Authenticity and Ethics gives us strong guidance and then using them to interpret into other things. For example, take ethics. We won't reduce the price of Easter eggs before Easter, so in other words I won't penalise my best customers who bought their Easter eggs early by selling them at a reduced price, just because we messed up slightly on a stock level for a particular Easter egg. So, it's more painful, but it's the right thing to do. Ethics means treating our customers fairly.

So, we're not like some fashion retailers who put their winter coats on sale before winter is over. That can only be a short-termism management approach that's crept in that will ultimately hurt them, but other retailers will be doing the same thing and there are many such examples of that.

Then there's authenticity which, for us, means being cocoa-led which then leads to using less sugar and more cocoa, which leads to a whole product approach. We articulated what the values mean and what we have to think about as a consequence. So, for example, we might want to do a fun product which would certainly sell because it's got Hotel Chocolat on it, but if it doesn't tick all of those boxes we've defined under our values then we won't do it. Yes, it might sell for a couple of years, but it's at the cost of our goodwill and we might make £100,000 profit out of that, but it will cost £500,000 in terms of brand goodwill. So, that clarity of definition makes it quite easy.

You're saying that the ethics theme continues within authenticity. You constantly look for the right thing by both your customers and your brand and what you stand for.

Definitely. I think that running a highly profitable and socially responsible and ethical business is not incompatible and that's a message that I try and get out as much as possible.

Having an ethical approach incentivises the right behaviours more and, as a result, we're recruiting and retaining better people, our people are working harder because we have a moral dimension to what we're trying to do and they are really compelled by that, compared to an approach all about just profit-maximising where tomorrow is forgotten about and customers are forgotten about because we'll make more profit this year. But what will happen in the subsequent years?

So, one leads to the other. Focusing on the long-term sustainability and being true to your values first and foremost means that, lo and behold, the profit follows.

Yes. My biggest thrill is protecting culture, protecting the brand values, making sure people are getting training on what they are and why they are important. The behaviours of an organisation are key and making sure those behaviours are as healthy as possible. Showing the right behaviours as a leadership team too and us demonstrating that every day.

Leaders that are living the values.

Exactly!

Could you give an example?

We've got so many examples of where we've taken on people who we just like because they have the right values, then we help them and train them to have the know-how. We've also recruited people from another business being unsure about them culturally, but assuming they must know a lot and it's never worked out.

When we opened Rabot 1745 in Borough Market here, for example, the first six months were a nightmare because I didn't actually fully apply what I've been saying. I thought I'd done enough in terms of menu, concept, products, then I'd assumed that what I needed now is operational know-how from experts in the industry sector.

So, I recruited a really good general manager, a really good restaurant manager and barman who came from best of breed businesses and I said "Just apply your know-how with our differentiated concept and that should work," and it didn't. It turns out we have a different operational methodology as well; we don't just think differently, we do things differently too. They tied themselves up in knots applying their model to our context and it just failed.

The general manager that we have now used to run a gastro pub and has a great attitude. He's running this site which has a restaurant, a bar, a café, a chocolate shop, as well as making chocolate too and he's doing a fantastic job.

Your chocolatier in the shop, Louise, was telling me earlier that she previously worked in a shop in Borough Market. When you recruited her, you knew that she understood the culture of Borough Market and how different it is here.

It appears that the culture in Borough Market is quite special in many ways. Many from the outside looking in might come here and see that you too sell food, drink and gifts, the same as many others in the market, so you are in competition. However, I understand that Rabot 1745 is the hub for the market traders themselves and it's central to the Borough Market community.

A hub – exactly. This is very community-based. We buy our bread from the bread stall just downstairs and we don't view each other as competitors. On the contrary, we try to support each other. It's very easy to take a dog in a manger approach and that just does not work, particularly somewhere like this where it is very community-based. There's a whole culture within the market. If you're out of that then you may as well not be in the market, but if you're in you really feel the warmth of it and it helps so much.

How necessary was it for you to understand and immerse yourself in the detail of Borough Market culture in order to get the brand positioned correctly here?

Well, we started our first foray into the cocoa bar concept across the road in a smaller site. We had the cocoa estate in St. Lucia and I came to realise that cocoa had been side-lined by focusing on chocolate and yet there was a whole world of possibility around cocoa too.

We were looking around for a site in London to test out the idea of the cocoa bar, reconstructing the hard core of cocoa drinks. I was looking around some sites in London and this smaller site came up in Borough Market. My agent showed it to me and I said "Yes, this is brilliant," and he said "It's not as easy as that, Angus. To get into the market you've got to pitch to get into the market and they've got to approve you and there are around 50 people going for every site."

So, I got in touch with the head of the market to find out what I needed to do and he told me, so I worked a proposal up and did the pitch and we got it. They were very keen to point out to me that "We don't want you to just disappear over the horizon. We back people with passion, you seem to have it, we like your vision and we want to see you around and know that you are on it." So, I said yes.

And after about three years at our smaller site in Borough Market we knew that the cocoa restaurant concept in St. Lucia really worked and we wanted to bring it to the UK. I'd got to know the market people pretty well by then and we'd built up a good track record with our cocoa shack and wanted to try something bigger. So, I approached them for a bigger site and they said there's not much happening.

I must have asked the head of the market about ten times and eventually he said "There might be something coming up, it's not there right now, but get your coat." So, we walked around and stood across the road from here and he pointed to here. He said "When this railway bridge is finished by Network Rail, they are building an office for me here on instruction of the previous head of the market, would that interest you?"

And he said that if you can satisfy us then you can have this site. There were a lot of twists and turns, including getting permission from the market to build the outdoor dining terrace overlooking the market.

So, that was a classic case of great opportunities coming your way when you are respectful and build the brand values and you get out what you put in really.

What do you believe it is about you that brings people on the journey?

I think people like my enthusiasm. I think I'm very straightforward and can energise them. I can be fun to work with and also at the same time I'm quite demanding. However, for the right sort of people, that's what they're looking for. And I have a strong ethical code in terms of how I deal with people so I've hardly fallen out with anybody who's worked for me and the people that I have, it's more about their emotional situation.

I make sure that when people have to leave the business, and I make it clear early on that at some point we agree that nothing's forever in business, and when the right time comes I'll have a straightforward conversation with you, and I'll make it elegant, but we've all got to agree that will have to happen at some point.

It's a conversation that our HR team has with all of our employees so that on day one, we prepare for exit. In business, skills and motivation are all aligned for a while. The business changes, you change and sometimes that drops out of alignment, and when that does let's not fall out over it or beat ourselves up. It just happens and it will be for the best and we'll work it out.

Frank and fearless conversations again...

Yes, very much. And that's come from really seeing how HR law sometimes forces people to treat other people like factors of production which dehumanises the whole thing. So, with the HR team we've agreed that the best way is to deal with that on day one so that we've already laid the foundations and it's part of our cultural values so that we can have an honest, professional, up-front conversation.

Preparing the ground work and then treating people like human beings...

Yes. Whenever we've had a problem with people needing to leave the business, the biggest antagonistic factor is going from being part of a team on the inside track to suddenly, for whatever reason, you're on the outside and we have to deal with you through this HR code which has no warmth and it's like being a non-person that we don't know anymore. We see you as a potential problem which makes them feel that they have to *be* a potential problem.

So, we try to have those conversations the human way, with respect and appreciating that we've had a lot of good years together and let's not spoil that. Life's too short to fall out over something like that.

Looking back, what other significant personal learning has there been that has unlocked the success of your business?

This is not anything cultural or brand-related per se, but more about functional skills. I think the utmost priority is to be given clear and timely financial information. I can and have run the business on instinct and I think I've been too forgiving in the past for slow, caveated financial information.

Last year we employed a top class CFO and he is very effective. He's shown me what I could've had years ago possibly and I really regret not having somebody as good as him around me earlier as I think we could've driven harder and faster if we'd had that information already.

So, I would say make no compromise on having one version of the truth out properly and communicated in a really simple way. You could have a thick dossier of data, but what does it say? What should we be doing? My CFO highlights areas and asks questions. For example, our seasonal sales against Thornton's are up which might mean that we are better than them at seasonal, or it might be that they are better than us at non-seasonal. What do you think it is? And it's the sort of discussion we have which is good for the business.

That timely and sensitive finger on the pulse, not just looking at historic numbers, but using forward-looking, interpretive data...

Yes. There's data and there's data. There's data which is a hotchpotch that nobody can see the wood for the trees from, and then there's data that somebody has sifted through and found the nuggets in, and that's what I'm interested in.

I don't need all the answers. I just need the main trends to get curious about. That's where you start making new actions, new decisions, and building opportunities. We've been very good on piloting the business on instinct for a very long time, but I now realise what we could've done if we'd had a big dollop of proper data alongside the instinct. We could've probably done things faster and better.

When you spot new opportunities, is your approach incremental e.g. test it, measure it and refine it?

We're not big on doing customer surveys and things first. We tend to do more live testing and that's because we have a direct relationship with our customers. Our normal way is, we come up with an idea, get early input, find a way to bring it to the market in a risk-contained way, watch and observe it, and either build or kill it at that point. So, we couldn't launch it to our customers if we didn't 80% believe it was going to work.

We never ask somebody else to verify our idea for us before we do it such as getting management consultants to come in to write a report that's going to cover us. That'll never happen in Hotel Chocolat. I tend to think of that approach as mediocre, fearful management from a defensive position.

If you had 30 seconds to give one final nugget of advice to other entrepreneurs and business owners, what would it be?

I'd say that in any business you can make it brand-led. If you're a service business or a welding business there's always a chance to make it brand-led. I think that if you can create a brand, that's going to lead to a stronger culture. It will then differentiate you in the market-place a lot more so, as well as having brilliant products and brilliant execution, you also have the brand that gives you the X factor.

It's well worth creating and investing in that brand and committing to living by it, so get a bit of brand wow into your business which is underpinned by your culture and living the values. A lot of people think that getting a great brand is using a design agency to think of a whizzy name and a letterhead. No, that's only 1% of it. The other 99% is: What does it feel like? What does it sound like? What does it taste like? How does it behave? What does it mean? All those questions have to be answered and lived by so it's a big commitment, but it gives you a solid framework.

Thank you very much indeed.

Very good to chat with you. You have great insight.

I love what I do and what you have shared here is so true to what I believe too. I work hard with businesses on 'What is it that you stand for? What's your legacy? How are you going to sustain that?' Otherwise it's success today, but what about tomorrow? It's the ability to grow that sustainable business that can operate without you. It needs others to be as passionate about your brand as you are. It's the only way in which the business will grow and live and take off without you being tied to it and it being tied to you.

It is, because you get tired, you have personal problems, you have health issues, you go off the boil. As a business owner you can't sustain 100% forever, so what's going to happen? If it's all down to you, your business will inevitably take a dip at some point. How many people rely on the business? Is it responsible? You're only human. It makes total and utter sense at a logical, financial and rational level that it has to be independent of you.

One of my greatest personal learnings was having qualified as an accountant and having come from that very logical, financially-driven focus on business, I quickly came to realise that you can have the best strategy in the world, but it's only a piece of paper. It's culture based on people, their behaviours and mind-set that are the difference to making it come alive.

When business owners keep tight hold of their baby it's through fear of others not having the same standards, losing control, often subconsciously preserving their position as the 'hero in the middle of the business' as you described it. It's from the fear of not being able to perform as a leader, the security of staying on as manager or doer. They then stifle the growth of their business and the people in it. Hence my qualifying as a leadership coach to support business owners through that.

Yes, they need a bit of something to get them over that hump. Where does that extra little bit of confidence come from? Some people might feel a little bit fraudulent about developing a brand and values for something that essentially doesn't exist. It's a set of values that you all decide to live by and yet how might you stand up and say this is something that you ought to come along on? It's like the fear of standing in the playground shouting "Who's going to be on my team?", turning around and there's nobody there. Everyone has a fear of that and that's where you come in to say that this really does work. There's the scientific management stuff, but it's the brand, values and culture that's going to make the business that much more exciting.

Yes, I agree. Thank you very much, Angus. It's been inspirational to meet you.

In brief

If you want you and your business to thrive, don't be the 'hero in the middle of your business', eternally busy, exhausted and stuck in the doing. Who else will truly share your passion and compel others to be involved if you don't?

Separate the issues and opportunities of alternative courses of action open to the business and have frank and fearless conversations. This can lead to faster growth.

Remember to keep it simple at all times. Refine communication as much as possible and then go back and refine again so that your messages are clear, simple and compelling.

To achieve brand-led success, you must become a master of different themes and an expert in a different array of fields. Understand that your brand means something with its own identity and pulse. Remember you are building it for long-term success, not a short-term gain.

Maintain strong ethics as an organisation. Be loyal to your customers and they will be loyal to you. Treat your suppliers right and they will do right by you. Being true to your values and goodwill will not be compromised at the expense of short-term gain.

Being a socially responsible and ethical business whilst making a profit is achievable, but not all ventures are an instant success. The original internet chocolate retailing business ChocExpress took ten years to refine. Rabot 1745 took six months to start moving smoothly as well as a complete overhaul of the management team.

Having people who share your values and whose attitude aligns and then training them up works. Employing knowledge experts in a particular field or for skills first and foremost, but who don't have the right alignment individually, does not.

Never compromise on the financial information that you have available. Having financial information with one version of the truth, distilled for the nuggets of key information contained within all the data and communicated in a really simple way will enable you to drive harder and faster.

Lastly, always remember to create, invest and live by your brand. If you fully commit to it, lead with it and role model it, you will have a solid framework for all decisions and a business that will stand the test of time!

Ever since our Tasting Club was founded in 1998 we've aimed to send exciting, original and innovative chocolates to our customers every month. As you can imagine, keeping 100,000 chocolate-loving members of our tasting club satisfied with a different selection every month means a great deal of chocolate recipes to create.

Experience a different side of Hotel Chocolat at our restaurants and cafes. Book a table at our stylish restaurants in London and Leeds and savour unique dishes inspired by the best of West Indian and modern British cuisine, enhanced with the subtle savoury spice of roasted cocoa.

Hotel Chocolat is the ultimate gift destination for chocolate gifts and luxury presents for birthdays, anniversaries, celebrations, commiserations, or even apologies! Or, create your own chocolate gift box and we'll pack it all together in a stunning black box, Hotel Chocolat ribbon and a gift tag with your personal message written inside ready in as little as two hours from store or same-day delivery to your door within hours should you need it.

Or learn the noble art of chocolate making with our experiences and events at The School of Chocolate cocoa vaults in the heart of London's Covent Garden.

Please visit our website at www.hotelchocolat.com to experience all that we have to offer !

Keith Paxman: "Don't be fearful... grasp the opportunity and run with it"

 Praxis42 was born in 2001 and the management team worked together for many years before that as the occupational health, safety and environment function for a FTSE 100 communications company.

Today they employ over 40 people in the UK who continue to deliver a professional service to national and international customers. Staff share common values, aspirations and core competencies to meet the needs of their very varied customer base which includes Monsoon, Everything Everywhere and Enterprise Inns.

The company structure, with advisers across the UK, enables Praxis42 to provide the very best health and safety, fire safety and environment support for large corporates, thus ensuring that the end product suits the ever-changing needs of their customers.

I spoke with Keith Paxman, Managing Director and one of the founding Directors of Praxis42.

Thanks for being involved, Keith. I look forward to hearing your story so far...

If we start just before the creation of Praxis42 in 2000. I was Head of Health, Safety and Environment at a corporate global business, Cable & Wireless, a telecoms organisation with activities throughout the world. I started initially in a subsidiary company, Mercury Communications, and moved my way up and built a team, but unfortunately around about 2000, not long after the .com bubble burst and things got a little bit tough in the sector, Cable & Wireless found themselves in a difficult place and needed to reduce headcount and manage costs.

I was given the opportunity to outsource my team, form my own business and then provide that service back to Cable & Wireless. After just a very short bit of thinking time, I seized that opportunity, engaged then four of the senior people in my team and formed the business with the five of us initially, myself as Managing Director and a team of four directors. Most of the team came with us and we formed this business which we called Praxis42.

Great name! How did it come to be?

We sat down and decided we needed to have a name that was a little different to what might be expected in our area of work. We went through a long list of alternatives, one of which was Praxis which loosely means turning theory into practice. The second was 42 which is from the *Hitchhikers Guide to the Galaxy* and is the solution to life, the universe and everything. Then, suddenly putting them both together, Praxis42 sounded not too silly and a little bit different and we seized on that and tested it with friends and family and they didn't think it was too silly either. It then stuck and it has stood the test of time, I think. We've made a bit of a name for ourselves as well. With our new company name, we then had three months to set it up, negotiate our exit opportunity and then we were up and running. It was a new journey for us. Although we had been revenue-earning within the business by providing our services to other organisations, we were very much in the forefront of the mobile telecoms market, providing services over the years to various providers. We had lots of experience, but we did need to diversify the business given its dependence on one main contract with Cable & Wireless and we needed to build it. From day one we acquired some new customers and continued to do so. We had then, and still have, two arms to the business, one as consultancy for health, safety and environment, and more importantly fire safety as well, and the other was providing our eLearning platform for health and safety courses. Both continue to be good revenue earners for us. Around 2005 we had a difficult couple of years where Cable & Wireless had shrunk so much that their services almost reduced to nothing and they took some services in-house again. They also took some of our people back and at that point we needed to significantly build the business. It helped us to hone in on the marketing and sales aspect of what we do and that then became a springboard for us to expand to where we are now, or where we were say a year ago, at which point we needed to reflect where we were going both as individuals and as a business. That's the point at which we needed to bring in somebody (an expert) to help us to see the way forward.

In moving from being an in-house service provider at a large company to being an external provider, how did you go about developing the additional skills needed to win your own work and run your own business?

Well, I think a number of ways really. I have previously studied to diploma level in business management, which I think gave me personally a sound business understanding. We did some work as a management team to develop individual skills and I ensured that we had professional support externally. I had a good lawyer, accountant and other support on the HR front when necessary. So, buying in those skills, rather than having them necessarily ourselves and, not that we needed a huge amount, but we did need enough to guide us. We managed to actually put something decent together and between us we've been very successful. So, if anybody fears that they haven't got the experience of running a business, don't be fearful, just grasp the opportunity and run with it.

It sounds as though you really concentrated on your core strengths, the things you were good at, and then bought in others you needed.

Exactly. And clearly, you learn by your successes, but you also learn by your mistakes as well. I can remember our accountant saying when you bring in somebody external into the business for a role such as sales and marketing, it's really over a year before you know if it was the right choice or not. And of course you do learn when you bring people in that sometimes it clicks and they work very well and sometimes it's a cost that you don't actually see a return on and it's time to move in another direction.

Yes, so keeping that antenna very sharp and focused. Just going back to that point at which you made the decision, is it correct that you were an employee for all of your previous careers?

Yes, I was.

Can you remember the moment you decided 'let's go for it' and what your thinking was?

I had always felt that I'd like to do my own thing and set up a consultancy, but of course when you have a young family and lots of commitments and you're on the conveyor belt of corporate world, it's not that easy to say 'That's it, I'm off.' So, this was actually a golden opportunity. It was handed to us and it was on the basis of providing the service back in to the same organisation, so of course you end up with great revenues in year one. In fact it was even more golden because we had the power in the deal which meant that we negotiated an up-front payment at the starting point, so we didn't even have a cash flow problem. What a wonderful way to start a business when you've got funding for your first few months, you've got a team around you that you know and respect and can rely on and you've got a golden customer. So, we had a really great business from the outset, rather than needing to build a business from nothing. So, perfect. As a result of that, the business in 15 years has never owed a penny to anybody and has been able to pay its way throughout, pay bonuses to our people and pay dividends to our shareholders. It's been a very, very successful enterprise.

There must have been times when you were trying to achieve something and were frustrated in your efforts, particularly in terms of where you want to take the business. Where do you see the gap between knowing what you want to do and actually getting there? What did you do?

The business was led by a team of people who were experienced and expert in their field as health and safety practitioners. At one point during 2005 revenues dipped and we needed to be not just directors, but also managers and undertake delivery as well. I think it's true to say that during that period the directors' focus had to be on delivery rather than managing and directing. That led to an approach within the team and a mind-set if you like that we need to get our hands dirty and we need to get in there with the team because of our experience. What that leads you to is a glass ceiling that you can't break through in terms of growing the business because you're relying on few people to do too much. At the same time, I think we became mindful that this isn't going to go on forever, one of the management team needed to take retirement and knew in advance that was going to be the case and we needed to rethink our approach. At that point we realised that if we wanted to grow we were going to need to let go.

What was your greatest personal learning within that journey?

I think it was probably that I needed to lead the management team to change our approach and thinking and daily activities. I needed to do that by leading by example, but I also needed to ensure that we engaged the right support to enable us to change our mind-set, to move the business on so that directors were directing so that we had a management structure in place and that we were also developing the individuals in our whole team, which by this time was around about the 40 mark in numbers and spread out throughout the UK. So, it was that awakening that if the business is going to continue, and to continue profitably, we need to make this move and the only way we can really achieve that is if I take a leadership role in doing that. At that point I looked externally into getting a person to help us in the same way, I guess, as we engaged the right people to help us in other aspects. It was somebody who could help us with change management.

There it is again; engaging externally and focusing on the strengths within your business. You also mentioned role-modelling. What did you notice needed to be done differently?

I found that in general most of the key decisions and also a huge number of minor daily business decisions were coming through my desk. Yes, it was fun and it was challenging, but it's what I've spent most of my career developing in terms of being able to deal with anything that is thrown at you. However, I knew there was also going to be a time when I wasn't going to be there, and indeed didn't want to be there, so if I didn't do something about that at some point the business could have been at risk. I also recognised of course that this wasn't just me, but my fellow directors were experiencing the same problems. There was also the recognition that we have a lot of good people working for us with lots of competencies and talents and we were in danger of not recognising those and not using them and potentially losing them. So, the whole of that really crystallised that we needed to let go, let the business grow and develop our people.

The key to you moving from doing to managing to leading was stepping out of problem solving and working at ground level and instead going up to the first floor and beyond and recognising the potential within your team...

Yes. We have a team of people that, apart from a few of those in our head office, work either from home or from customer sites and work on their own. All of them are very professional, but many of them actually work in isolation, very low maintenance, just get on with the job and actually we realised that some people have worked for us for quite a while and yet we didn't know them. We didn't know what their competencies and capabilities are. We know what is required of them and what they're demonstrating at the times when we touch what they're doing, but actually we knew all the experience certain people had, degrees in certain subjects or previous lifetimes and had experience in certain areas before we employed them. Yet we weren't making use of those, we were just asking them to do what we required of them and some have run their own businesses, some have been managers in other businesses and yet we weren't making use of that.

Knowing your people and knowing more about their journey and using their knowledge, skills and experience more widely was essential...

Yes, and also understanding what their motivators are, what their ambitions are and their aspirations. At some point you need to fully understand that and what we did with that was engaged somebody else externally who helped us to measure and understand that to explore a little bit more about what they were looking for and where they were going, and that led us to consider who was appropriate for manager positions looking after our teams, who was appropriate for account managing of a major customer, or account managing a smaller business customer which then enabled us to get them to do the day-to-day work and day-to-day management with guidance and support and direction from the directors.

It's been a great journey so far in terms of personally role-modelling leadership, stepping out of doing and enabling others to step in and, from that, creating opportunities for everybody...

Of course, yes. I think it's true to say we're still on the journey, we've still got a team of people that are feeling their way and we've still got directors who are in the process of letting go and need to let go some more, or sometimes need to bring it back in and need to flex their roles almost on a daily basis. It's working though, the business now is at a place when it is only limited by our imagination and what we think we can do, but those limits are much wider and larger and further than they might have been a year or two ago.

What one further golden nugget of advice would you pass on to another business owner?

I would say don't be limited by what you think you can achieve. Find the right person to help you with that, whether that person is internal or external, but use the right people. Open your mind, really consider what your role within this is and what the role of your management team is within this and then just give it a go.

One thing that strikes me from your story is your ability to get higher perspective in terms of recognising what needs to be done. How would you say that you do that?

There are a number of areas in which you can take that perspective. One of them is on 'What's our key offering? What makes us different and separates us from our competitors?' That sort of approach. There's also the approach of 'How can we get the best out of our team individually?' and then moving onto things like 'What are our values?' So, I think you can have a higher level approach, but then you need to almost segment that into 'What is it that needs to be done in this business to take us forward?' So, that I think is one of the keys; stepping away, finding time and not being involved in doing. Letting go allows you to do that. Finding time to think things through to take an objective, rather than a subjective view on things and trusting those around you to get on with what you want and the business needs from them and giving them the freedom to do it and go for it. I would also say don't expect it to happen overnight, but stick with it and the benefits will come. After our period of investment we are now seeing the growth in revenues and customers that we thought were ambitious targets only a few months ago.

Thank you very much indeed.

You're welcome!

In brief

Know your own strengths as individuals and as a board and bring in external support to assist as and when you need it.

Show others the way by leading by example, being open to shifting your mind-set and doing things differently and, in so doing, you'll see others change too.

Move from the comfort of problem solving, which might make you feel good, but is capping business growth, to enabling others to flourish and empowering them to do it for themselves.

Know all of your employees individually as people. Be aware of their skills, history and aspirations and use that knowledge to create the right opportunities within the business for them and you. This will enable you to engage the right person for the right job by not being limited by your own thinking.

Take a step back and time out to objectively review the business with a higher perspective. Then commit the time to make change happen by showing and trusting others to do more for themselves, being readily available to offer your support when needed without overcrowding and allowing individuals to grow.

We recognise that health and safety management can often be seen as a challenge. Organisations often don't know where to start to understand legislation or best practice and want a balanced view on risk.

Praxis42's specialism is sensible and pragmatic risk management. Over the years we have dealt with a wide range of businesses and sectors and are confident we can help with your occupational health, safety, fire and environment needs.

We can help you choose the exact service, training course or strategy that you need to meet your legal and moral obligations and develop a comprehensive compliant management system.

Please visit our website for further information: www.praxis42.com

Angela Dellar: "Keep it simple"

I've always loved business, understanding why some businesses achieve great success and others don't to the same degree, and distilling my learning into simple, practical tools which I share with clients to help them succeed.

Simply put, business success is the ability to generate enough money, in particular cash. A strong business is like a three-legged stool with the legs being:

1. Business know-how or business IQ: (i) **what** you do, for whom and why, (ii) how that generates enough money and (iii) where you are going now and in the future.

2. People know-how or emotional intelligence (EQ): **who** you are being (i) individually, (ii) as a team and (iii) culturally as a business to grow positive, long-term relationships.

3. Action! Regular, focussed action towards strategic goals: **how** you get there.

Simple, but not easy.

Business IQ: What you do

Business IQ ensures that what you are doing and where you are going has the ability to generate enough money. The key ingredients include:

- Doing what you are really good at.

- Having enough customers willing to buy and able to pay.

- Positioning the business to be different so that customers come to you rather than the competition.

- Consistently delivering that difference to customers to meet their needs around time, cost and quality.

- Sound management information (financial and non-financial) to give factual validation.

- Having external perspective, identifying and taking advantage of potential opportunities.

- Ensuring that risks are managed.

When a business grows to a certain level – typically £750,000 turnover or five employees – it needs the MD to shift into a higher gear in order to grow further. Rather than being consumed by the day-to-day delivery, the MD must lead the change by giving the team the capability and the confidence to run the day-to-day, whilst maintaining and growing what has made the business successful to date – its key core values and culture.

The business' processes also need to change gear, becoming streamlined, standardised and automated to enable consistent customer service.

Finally, management information also needs to shift up a gear enabling the MD to keep a 'finger on the pulse', having confidence that customers and the team are happy and the business performance is healthy, without having a 'finger in the pie' of the day-to-day operations.

Business EQ: Who you are being

Being conscious of your thinking, the emotions and behaviours it provokes, and being able to regulate them, is called **emotional intelligence** or **EQ**. In short, EQ enables you to behave in a way that maximises your chances of success, and enables others to do likewise.

People working in a business where there is strong EQ support and collaborate with each other, and the atmosphere is one of open and frank conversations, clear expectations and mutual trust and respect. It's a bit like the atmospheric conditions in a greenhouse where the right conditions attract and retain good people and when it's not so good, the business and the people in it don't achieve their fullest potential.

The MD often has the greatest influence on the atmospheric conditions in a business. Where consumed in day-to-day action, solving operational problems, tactically reacting to issues and then frequently changing direction, they are holding the business and people back. The often unconscious thinking that leads to what are essentially defensive behaviours includes:

- the fear of failure,

- the struggle to delegate ('others don't do it like I do'),

- guilt at not being in the muck and bullets of day-to-day busyness,

- fear of being unable to do this new role well,

- the worry of 'What if people don't like me when I have to be 'the boss', not one of the team?'.

The MD is not alone in thinking this way. To varying degrees, we all think like this due to our in-built survival instincts of fight, flight or freeze. Business growth is stifled unless the MD and the team understand and regulate these defensive behaviours so that everyone and everything is pulling in the same direction. The good news is that EQ can be grown at any point throughout our lifetime when we become the open-minded observers of our own behavioural movies. More on that later.

Growing EQ creates a productive environment and has distinct financial benefits too. A business generating £1 million on the bottom line is worth approximately £1.5 million when the MD is consumed with day-to-day delivery. That same business, still generating £1 million, is typically worth upwards of £4.5 million (depending on the sector) when it is fully independent of the business owner.

Some people believe that emotions at work are generally a negative, and so shun the concept of emotional intelligence. What they fail to realise is that higher emotional intelligence makes the workplace calmer, more productive and more profitable. Negative behaviours, such as operational silos, which give rise to both 'them and us' issues and a lack of full collaboration across business areas (or within a board), are substantially reduced. What you may view as 'fluffy emotional stuff' gives measurable competitive advantage by attracting the right people to your business, and is a commercial necessity if your goal is to maximise the valuation of the business.

Action! Regular, focussed action towards strategic goals

The third essential ingredient for strong and sustainable business growth centres on taking regular, focussed action towards strategic goals, measuring the outcome of that action and refining it in the light of events. Great strategies that never make it off the page are about as useful as an unused gym membership in getting you fit. 90 minutes each day is all it takes, and if you think you haven't got time, read on.

Having asked every MD interviewed to share their personal learning that has had the most profound impact on their business success, it's only right that I share two of my own which directly relate to two of the three legs of strong business described above.

My first learning: The daily 90 minute strategic session

"We are what we repeatedly do. Excellence is therefore a habit." - Aristotle

The habit of 90 minutes per day of uninterrupted focus on actioning strategic goals is the most common attribute of high performing business leaders. I first learnt about it from a book by Nigel Botterill who learnt it from Martin Howey - who probably learnt it from someone else!

The science bit is that just as our sleep has different flows, so does our energy during the day. These are called Ultradian Performance Rhythms. Our body's natural energy cycle flows in 90-120 minute waves of peak performance, each followed by 20 minutes of rest. Performers and athletes train to this cycle. There will be one point in the day where you are absolutely at your peak. Mine is around 7:30am. If I exercise, shower and eat before I start, my productivity during those 90 minutes and throughout the day nearly doubles.

Work out when your best time of day is. Use it for focussed action, and guard it fiercely.

Before I start those 90 minutes:

- I begin with the end in mind. What do I want to get out of my 90 minutes? Why is that important? How does it move me towards my larger goals?

- I work backwards and break my 90 minutes into four 20 minute chunks with 10 minutes at the end. I prioritise each chunk, ensuring that it's work that only I can do and delegate the rest.
- The unbreakable rule is that these 90 minutes cannot be interrupted. I need solitude, quiet and no clutter so I turn off the phone (mobile and landline) and emails so that I can completely focus.

During:

- I set a timer (not on my phone, otherwise I'm distracted by texts, messages and mail) and work for 20 minutes. At the end of that session I evaluate progress before moving ahead with my next 20 minute goal. Having a deadline really helps me focus and avoid perfecting.
- What can go wrong will go wrong. I have to roll with the unexpected interruptions and carry on.
- Stick to the plan.

After:

- Stop. Take stock of what I've achieved and write it down. Take two minutes to reflect. What am I proud of? What strengths did I use? What made it possible to do that? How can I use that more? This releases endorphins so grows the mental association between my 90 minutes and the feel good factor, makes me more conscious of

what works for me, and motivates me to keep up the good work.
- Plan the next day's 90 minutes. Look at it before signing off for the day so that my subconscious brain will work on it overnight.
- Take 15 minutes to rest and recuperate.

After my 90 minutes, I feel really good about what I've achieved and it gives me more energy for the rest of the day.

You can use the same technique at other points in the day for routine day-to-day work too.

I use the urgent/important grid developed by Stephen Covey to prioritise what I need to do. Vital to moving the business forward is the top-right corner – important but not urgent projects. Those valuable things you need to do but otherwise will never get around to. I aim to include these in my daily 90 minute slot.

It's important to build consistency:

- Know why you're doing it and keep that in the front of your mind.

	Important	
Urgent	Important and urgent Delegate as low as possible. Determine relative priorities.	Important but not urgent Strategic projects. Will reduce the important and urgent volume. Complete in your first 90 min slot of the day
	Not important but urgent Things like interruptions, some calls, emails, meetings that should be cut out where possible. Beware of comfort tasks.	Not important and not urgent Bin it!
	Not important	**Not urgent**

- Stay proactive. Don't slip into reactive things, such as emails.
- Avoid time wasters – people who drain your energy and your time (energy vampires), or comfort tasks such as clearing the email inbox or getting involved in the doing.
- Have fun and recognise your achievements.

My second learning: growing my business emotional intelligence (EQ)

A simple tool that helped me to grow my EQ was learning to respond rather than react. In the traditional chain of events, something happens, you react and that reaction can lead to an unintended outcome. Your reaction is completely spontaneous, and happens before you know it.

A significant personal learning for me was that there's a magical six seconds in between that event happening and your reaction that follows. Those six seconds, the time that a pedestrian crossing beeps for, provide an opportunity to develop your pause button.

Learning to press the pause button gives you the ability to freeze-frame the situation and gain a higher perspective. In the space of a breath you can look down and ask yourself, 'What's the most important outcome here?'

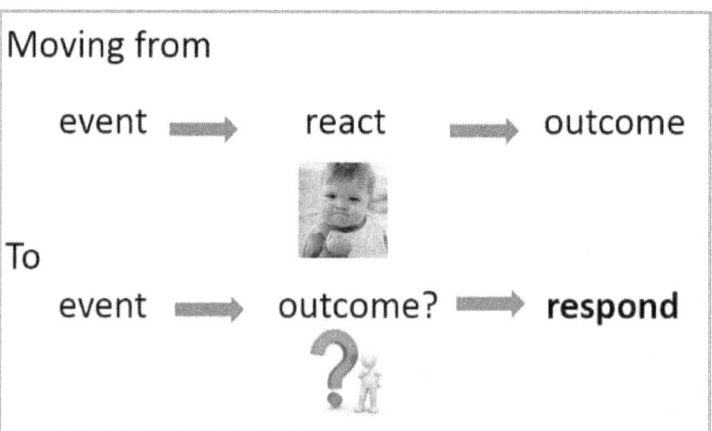

Consciously moving the outcome from the end of the chain to the middle gives a powerful opportunity. It's the opportunity to choose, to decide how best to respond with consciously chosen behaviour that takes you towards your goals rather than spontaneously reacting.

The most effective outcome in driving business growth is creating a positive culture with shared values, disseminated control and decisions, and people who feel confident and capable in what they are doing.

Everyone can use this simple technique and it makes an incredible difference in all aspects of life, including parenting teenagers (she says from experience!).

I've also learned to increase the length of the pause by developing my awareness of the triggers that send me into a spontaneous reaction. Like most business owners, I like control, have high standards and am driven to achieve high levels of performance. I've noticed that many of my triggers stem from these preferences which have been fuelled by the sayings of my youth such as 'don't care, was made to care', which I, unconsciously, can take too far.

I now very consciously distinguish between caring *about* and caring *for* the outcome or the person. Caring about is a good balance. I care about what we get and this is a partnership where I do half the work and you do half the work. When I move into caring *for* I go beyond that healthy balance into taking responsibility for the outcome or the person which takes me away from my business goals.

Another saying of my youth is 'if a job's worth doing, it's worth doing well'. I'm driven to do the best I can which can make me a perfectionist at certain times, particularly with the written word. The right balance is good standards and being professional. Perfection is insatiable - impossible to achieve.

When I'm perfecting I draft, edit, rework and edit again, leaving too little time for other essential tasks and so end up working late and under increasing pressure of impending deadlines. When I'm perfecting it's as if I'm being driven by some external force with the outcome being exhaustion, stress, a lack of fun and procrastination. Moving from reacting to responding has been liberating.

To move forward, I have accepted that I am accountable for my behaviours and made small shifts in my thinking giving dramatically different outcomes. Focussing on the higher, more long-term outcome rather than having an immediate, spontaneous reaction for something to be the best it can be / the need to win / be heard / have the last word, opens up new options. I'm calmer, no longer frustrated at the same thing happening time and again and I'm driving forward rather than tripping myself and others up.

I don't always get it right and sometimes I don't notice when I need to respond rather than react (for example, if I'm tired). When things go astray I give myself time for my emotions to calm and ask myself, however uncomfortable, 'What could I have done differently to get a different outcome?' and choose to learn from it.

Leadership coaching has been a powerful way of enabling clients to do likewise. Seeing the small shifts in thinking when they unlock themselves, their team and their business is very rewarding. When more people in the business are able to consciously respond rather than react defensively it puts both their personal and business growth on steroids. It accelerates how they perform together, things become simpler and the results on all levels are outstanding.

On the importance of committing:

"Desire is the key to motivation, but it's the determination and commitment to unrelenting pursuit of your goal – a commitment to excellence – that will enable you to attain the success you seek." Mario Andretti

Commit to 90 minutes and to responding rather than reacting; make them habits, and I guarantee you'll be amazed at the progress you make.

In brief

Business success is the ability to generate enough money - in particular cash - over the long term, based on:

1. Business acumen (business IQ).
2. Creating the environment to get the best out of yourself and your people (emotional intelligence or EQ).
3. Taking 90 minutes of action towards your goals every day.

Leaders need to move out of the day-to-day and into the strategic. For a business owner wanting to maximise their business's valuation, a further gear change is needed to move them into the role of Chairman, delegating responsibility for strategic delivery.

The best systems, processes and business ideas are limited without emotionally intelligent leadership - the ability to bring people on the journey so they want to be a part of the new world.

Master the skill of moving from reacting to responding. Grow your self-awareness to know yourself better. This will allow you to self-regulate your behaviour.

The people in a business with strong EQ feel that they are on the same side and part of something special. They support and collaborate and the atmosphere is one of open and frank conversations, clear expectations and mutual trust and respect.

Strong EQ is the cornerstone of attracting and retaining good people.

The most important action for an MD is to share key values, disseminate control and decisions, grow a positive culture with strong EQ and to make themselves redundant from operational delivery and then, for the business owner MD, strategic delivery.

Be conscious of distinguishing between caring *about* the outcome or the person, and caring *for*.

There will be one point in the day where you are absolutely at your peak. Find yours, use it and guard it fiercely.

Perfection is insatiable. It's something you can never achieve and unless you're aware, you'll just keep driving and pushing for it. You will never get there and will burn yourself and any fun out along the way.

About the Author

Angela Dellar started her career by qualifying as an accountant with KPMG where she gained wide exposure to a variety of sectors: oil, insurance, brewing, petroleum, professional services, graphic designers, construction and even an abattoir, to name a few.

She loves getting under the skin of any business by having a walk-through from end to end and distilling the business into its key drivers, including the leadership qualities that enable high performance individuals and teams.

From KPMG she left practice for a board role in the Property Services division of Atkins, the construction consultants, with shared responsibility for setting the strategy, business planning and implementation.

Working closely with her team, the board and the managers in the business, she grew the financial and commercial capability by ensuring that the 'numbers side' was simplified, that bright spots could be seen and replicated and the financial impact of actions understood.

From Atkins Angela progressed to Marsh, a global insurance and reinsurance broker, where she continued to have board-level management responsibility, including strategy and business positioning, and also new challenges in change management, project management and more detailed process efficiency. As Head of UK Change Management,

Angela specialised in the human side of change, including organisation design, training and development and cultural integration of a European client base.

During the deep recession of 2009 Angela fulfilled her dream of starting her own business. In the early stages her business focused on strategy, growth maximisation through business positioning and change management for the small to medium sized businesses that she had loved working with at KPMG.

She then recognised that she had varying degrees of success dependent on the mind-set of the MD and so qualified in behavioural change as a Leadership Coach with the International Coaching Federation. Peter Drucker once said, "Culture eats strategy for breakfast." The best systems, processes and business strategy will never make it off the page without leaders creating the right culture; the ability to bring people on the journey so they want to be a part of the new world. By positively influencing small shifts in mind-set, Angela enables dramatic change in the ability of leaders to grow the right environment for success whilst enabling accountability for taking action towards the goals identified.

Equipped in all three key areas of business success - business IQ, business EQ and change management to take regular focused action to deliver strategy - Angela thoroughly enjoys supporting MDs to grow themselves, their teams and their business, yielding tangible results in a short space of time.

Thank you's

Firstly, and most importantly, I'd like to thank those that have given up their precious time to create such a useful resource. Without their generosity this book would not have been created. Without their honesty and openness, the learning in this book would not be as rich for others.

So, a very big thanks to the following highly successful founding entrepreneurs and leaders:

- Peter Jarvis, Contechs
  www.contechs.co.uk

- Rowan Gormley, Naked Wines and Majestic Wines
  www.nakedwines.co.uk

- Dr Louise Beaumont, GLI Finance
  www.glifinance.com

- Alan Ridealgh, Muntons
  www.muntons.com

- Russ Stilwell, RSE Building Services
  www.rsebuildingservices.com

- Angus Thirlwell, Hotel Chocolat
  www.hotelchocolat.com

- Keith Paxman, Praxis42
  www.praxis42.com

I'd also like to say a huge thank you to one of my mentors, Graham McGregor of Twomac Consulting. I have tried and tested Graham's marketing services and strategies and they have always proved to be hugely successful. This book was inspired by the hugely popular special report that Graham offers his own clients called "The Unfair Business Advantage." This report by Graham is outstanding and I highly recommend that you get a copy. It's available for free at www.theunfairbusinessadvantage.com.

Enjoy, learn, and put it into action. To your success!

P.S. Why the swift on the front cover?

As a group, swifts are the fastest of all birds in level flight. Their wings are long, narrow and superbly adapted for fast flight. Even their forked tail is closed to a point during flight for extra efficiency. Everything about this bird is designed for

speed and height! They almost never land, except at their nest sites, doing everything on the wing (including sleeping, eating and mating). They drink by gliding over smooth water and taking sips.

They also have an amazingly clever adaptation. Food can be scarce in bad weather. The chicks can go cold and torpid and survive for days without food, then regain weight rapidly once supplies resume. Most baby birds can't do this and would simply die within hours.

The relevance for business? Taking swift action, adapting to the environment and growing resilience are all essential to success.

Copyright notices

Copyright © 2015 by Angela Dellar, Apricot Business Growth.

All rights reserved.

No part of this publication may be reproduced or transmitted in any form or by any means, mechanical or electronic, including photocopying and recording, or by any information storage and retrieval system, without permission in writing from the publisher.

Requests for permission or further information should be e-mailed to angela.dellar@apricotbusinessgrowth.co.uk

Website: www.apricotbusinessgrowth.co.uk

Published by Apricot Business Growth

Legal notices

While all attempts have been made to verify information provided in this publication, neither the author nor the publisher assumes any responsibility for errors, omissions or contrary interpretation of the subject matter.

This publication is not intended for use as a source of legal or accounting advice. The publisher wants to stress that the information contained herein may be subject to varying local laws or regulations. All users are advised to retain competent counsel to determine what local laws or regulations may apply to the user's particular business.

The purchaser or reader of this publication assumes responsibility for the use of these materials and information. Adherence to all applicable laws and regulations, both national, local, governing professional licensing, business practices, advertising and all other aspects of doing business in the United Kingdom or any other jurisdiction is the sole responsibility of the purchaser or reader.

The author and publisher assume no responsibility or liability whatsoever on the behalf of any purchaser or reader of these materials.

Any perceived slight of specific people or organisations is unintentional.

www.ingramcontent.com/pod-product-compliance
Lightning Source LLC
Chambersburg PA
CBHW060901170526
45158CB00001B/452